# A Guide for Caregivers of Aging Parents with Alzheimer's

Copyright © 2013, Ellen Gerst
All Rights Reserved.
Phoenix, Arizona
www.LNGerst.com

No part of this book may be reproduced or transmitted in any form or by any means, electronic or mechanical, including photocopying, recording or by any information storage and retrieval system, without the written consent of the author, except where permitted by law except in the case of brief quotations embodied in critical articles and reviews.

Disclaimer: This publication is for informational and inspirational purposes only and is not to be construed as professional counseling advice.

ISBN: 978-1494402402

---

Gerst, Ellen
A Guide for Caregivers of Aging Parents with Alzheimer's Words of Assistance, Comfort and Inspiration

# Words of Assistance, Comfort and Inspiration

Ellen Gerst

# Table of Contents

## Words of Assistance for Caregivers

| | |
|---|---|
| Introduction | 1 |
| The Pick-Up Sticks Theory on Life and Loss | 5 |
| You Are NOT Alone | 8 |
| Duality: Burden or Blessing? | 10 |
| Love vs. Fear | 11 |
| How To Recognize Anger | 14 |
| Neutrality | 16 |
| Reflectively Respond vs. Reflexively React | 19 |
| W.H.A.M.! | 21 |
| Mom's Story | 25 |
| It Doesn't Have To Be Alzheimer's | 31 |
| Readjusting the Lens | 38 |
| How Memories Are Made | 40 |
| A Mechanism for Handling Repetition | 42 |
| Learning To Speak A New Language | 43 |
| Paranoia | 47 |
| Let A Therapist Be the Bad Guy | 51 |

## Words of Inspiration and Comfort for Caregivers

| | |
|---|---|
| Introduction | 55 |
| More Than Merely Existing | 57 |
| It's A New Game | 58 |
| What Kind of Advice Are You Receiving? | 59 |
| Take Care of Yourself | 61 |
| Making It All Better | 63 |
| Control Is An Illusion | 65 |

| | |
|---|---|
| Finding Your Power | 67 |
| Spring Always Follows Winter | 68 |
| Procrastination Gets A Bad Rap | 69 |
| Past, Present, Future | 70 |
| What Lies Beneath The Iceberg? | 72 |
| Life Isn't Black and White | 74 |
| Open Every Door | 75 |
| Filling Up Than Empty Feeling | 76 |
| The Gift of Pain | 78 |
| Looking At Life Through New Eyes | 79 |
| Responding To Loss | 80 |
| Handling Celebratory Events | 81 |
| The Longest Day | 82 |
| Growth | 83 |
| Quizzes vs. Final Exams | 84 |
| Finding The Harmony | 85 |
| What Is Life? | 86 |
| Look At The Small Picture | 87 |
| Is This How You Feel? | 88 |
| Finding That Comfortable Place | 89 |
| Moving Towards The Light | 90 |
| Feelings Of Loss Will Not Be Ignored | 91 |
| Can You Turn Off The Noise? | 92 |
| What Is The Truth? | 93 |
| Finding Optimism | 94 |
| It's Never Too Late To Change | 95 |
| The Mind-Body Wellness Connection | 96 |
| Is Busy-ness Your Coping Mechanism? | 97 |
| The Ups and Downs of Life | 98 |

| | |
|---|---|
| Finding Your Courage | 99 |
| Adapting To Change | 100 |
| Priceless! | 101 |
| Does Your Life Feel Like An Uphill Battle? | 102 |
| If Only … | 103 |
| Caregiving = A Time of Introspection | 104 |
| You're The Star of Your Own Show | 105 |
| Alethiology: The Study of Truth | 106 |
| Understanding The Cycle of Life and Death | 107 |
| Feeling Whole Again | 108 |
| Shun Stagnation | 109 |
| The Dual Nature of Loss | 110 |
| Regaining Your Focus After Loss | 111 |
| K.I.S.S.= Keep It Super Simple | 112 |
| Revitalize Your Zest For Living | 113 |
| Conclusion: Finding Grace | 115 |
| Author Bio and Contact Information | 117 |

# Introduction

If you are reading this book, you're probably in a similar situation as I find myself. I'm a baby boomer who is helping to care for a loved one with Alzheimer's. In my case, it's my -year-old mother.

How we may differ is that I'm also a grief and relationship coach, and I have had experience helping people deal with difficulties brought on by loss. Of course, it's a lot easier to offer assistance to others than to put these same suggestions to use in your own life. However, I try my best. In fact, that's one of the reasons why I write about the lens of loss and how it applies to caregiving: it's to constantly remind me about how I can best respond to my own difficult situations.

Perhaps you may be puzzled by my choice of the areas of expertise in which I specialize. On the surface, it might seem as if they don't fit together very well, but I beg to differ. You see, I think everything in life is about loss, and the better you're able to understand this subject, the more successful you'll be in navigating through it and be able to find renewal or experience a rebirth.

The cycle of loss and rebirth is one that is repeated throughout our life, with some losses being small (such as a disappointment) to others being monumental. And what's the best way to move through these losses – or really the rest of your life? It is with the support of those you love the best – the ones with whom you have the closest relationships.

I started digging into the intricacies of coping with loss due to my own tragic circumstances. Almost two decades ago, when I was in my late thirties, my first husband passed away without any warning. In those years, there wasn't much support for young widows and I certainly floundered, as most would do in a similar situation.

The main reason why this occurred is because society fails to adequately teach its members how to mourn. Why? Well, no one wants to talk about loss and how to cope with the subsequent grief because that means looking at things most would rather avoid. After all, it makes you confront your own mortality and that can be a scary proposition.

Although many of you may be familiar with loss – because as I said it comes in all different forms, some of which aren't recognized – not many know what to do with the nebulous feelings they may experience such as anger or lethargy.

Moreover, if you're in the midst of losing or have already lost a loved one, others *sort of* understand your circumstances and the feelings you're experiencing. And I say *sort of* because they want you to quickly get your emotions under control. Not so much for you, but because your loss makes them feel uncomfortable – that it might even be contagious and, if it could happen to you, it could happen to them too.

It's the same for other types of losses. Others might feel bad for you and say, *"Oh, you're so strong; I don't know how you do it."* However, they don't really want to hear the details about how you're suffering. Consequently, you may feel alone, isolated, think you're going crazy or believe that you're the only one that feels a particular way.

## Words of Assistance, Comfort and Inspiration

Feelings of loss and grief are certainly experienced as your parents age and if they become ill. When this occurs, the process of losing many things commences. For example, you may have feelings of loss about (1) the erosion of the foundation that parents provide that has always been your safety net; (2) the feelings of unconditional love and acceptance you've experienced and upon which you've come to rely; and (3) the natural idea of how the parent/child relationship works because now you're about to switch roles.

If you don't know anything about loss and grief because you've been lucky enough not to suffer much of it in your life, there's no reason you would recognize that many of the emotions you may be experiencing now are all about feeling bereft concerning your situation.

Accordingly, before I offer tips and thoughts on how to cope with some of the specific challenges you are tackling, I am going to provide a brief introduction on how to recognize and cope with loss and the natural grieving process that accompanies it.

*Words of Assistance, Comfort and Inspiration*

## THE PICK-UP STICKS THEORY ON LIFE AND LOSS

As I moved through my feelings of grief due to the loss of my late husband, I started to formulate my own theory on how life and loss works. I based this theory on the old childhood game of Pick-Up Sticks.

In this game, each participant holds many multi-colored sticks in her hand. The sticks are thrown up in the air and land scattered about. It's each player's job to pick up as many sticks as possible without disturbing or moving any of the others.

I want you to imagine that each stick represents a person, place, task, individual memory, or an event or circumstance. When you hold them tightly in your hand, you have a firm grip on all the parts of your life. As you journey forth through the life you have planned, you may hit a bump in the road – or even worse, a terrible tragedy. This "bump" or loss causes you to trip. As you fall, your hand opens, and your sticks fly up into the air and are strewn all over the place with some pieces more buried than others. As the days and months (and sometimes years) go by, you will attempt to pick up your sticks – or, as I like to call them, the threads of your life. This doesn't happen all at once; most likely, you will accomplish this task in stages.

At the inception of your loss, your world may seem so dark that you cannot even see where any of the sticks have flown. With a little bit of support, the light can start to stream back into your life – perhaps just enough so that you can gingerly pick up the sticks that are on the surface. These sticks represent the everyday chores you must complete. Despite your loss and/or difficult circumstances, life continues on and you must work, take care of yourself, your family, home, etc.

Now, you may notice that some of the sticks have rolled very far away. These might represent people who have deserted you, hold a negative attitude, or who make your difficulties all about them instead of offering support. It would take too much energy to pick those up, so you will let them go. Since you don't need extra negativity in your life, their absence can actually be beneficial to you.

The truth is that you may *never* pick up some of your sticks. These discarded sticks might represent things that weren't working in your old life or seem trivial and unimportant now, so there is no reason to include them in your new life.

However, there are still plenty of sticks left on the ground. There may be some that are hidden at the bottom of the pile and, if you try to pick these up too early without clearing some of the obstacles, you may encounter defeat. Additionally, you may feel that some of the sticks are too hard to pick up – even though they might be on the surface. You may decide to ignore or work around these until you feel ready to confront the issues they represent. Keep in mind, though, that to regain your equilibrium, you will eventually need to examine the dreaded sticks you may be avoiding.

When you have picked up all the appropriate sticks and arranged them into a pleasing configuration, you can consider that the major portion of your grief journey has been completed. As you examine the sticks in your hand, you might also notice a different formation. This is because the picture of your life has been greatly altered, so doesn't it make sense that the way the pieces of your life fit together should be altered too? This is exciting news because it means you have grown and evolved into the "new you" – a person who knows how to handle adversity and has developed the skills for enabling adaptation to new circumstances.

To further enrich your life, you will try to always remember the important lessons learned on your journey from darkness to light.

As you continue forward on your path of life, while encountering diverse experiences and people, you will have the opportunity to pick up new sticks and add them to your bouquet. And, as you slide them in, you may notice that the tight grip you previously had on your sticks is a little looser than it was before your loss.

One of the lessons learned is that no matter how tightly you hold onto the vision of your life as you know it, it can change in a moment. Staying loose, going with the flow, stopping to smell the roses – these ways of approaching life make it less of a struggle. Moreover, adopting this type of attitude allows you to remain in control of your life with the realization that, if the sticks would happen to fall out of your hand again, you possess the strength to pick them up and start again.

This idea is at the crux of the concepts that I will be discussing – how to change your perspective on loss to be able to accept the hardships and disappointments that come with your changing role as a caregiver, yet still be able to figure out a way to move forward with grace as you offer support and care to your aging parents.

## YOU ARE NOT ALONE

As I mentioned previously, loss can be very isolating. However, I want you to know that you're NOT alone – even when it feels that way.

Emerging feelings of isolation are often *self-imposed* because many have a tendency to push people away when they're hurting. They may feel like a burden to others, if they appear to be weak and in need of help. The truth is that this is the time when you require a support network the most, and friends and family are usually more than willing to reach out a helping hand. The rest is up to you because you need to *allow yourself to accept* the offered help. Keep in mind that it's your relationships with others that will provide the most assistance in coping with your situation.

When you keep all your emotions to yourself – tempered down and bottled up inside – you become a volcano that can literally explode at any moment. It's beneficial to air your feelings because they may sound different and less overwhelming when expressed aloud *vs.* having them only roll around in your brain. I call this the *bounce back* element, which provides a reality check and allows you to receive feedback from others who can help you to see possible resolutions to your issues.

Before you started your personal journey of caregiving, you may have heard about the difficulties others encountered. Your mind may have absorbed this information generically, but it's likely that you didn't pay much attention to it or retain it. Now that it's happening to you and your family, it's brand new and front and center in your consciousness.

## Words of Assistance, Comfort and Inspiration

The enormity of the task in front of you can seem overwhelming, and you may not even know where to begin. Some of the best ways to learn about what this undertaking is going to entail are as follows: completing your due diligence on caregiving and the different types of dementia; talking to professionals; and communing in a support group with those in similar situations.

Remember, along with *your* feelings of isolation and fear, your loved one is *also* feeling isolated and scared. It's probably going to be your job to allay these frightening emotions that can compound the effects of the disease.

Once your parent or other loved one has started the march towards dependence on you and others, it's a journey where there's no turning back. Even if they are in a stage where they're not totally aware of what's going on, they still probably know that a move out their own home means that they're relinquishing their independence, which they know will never be recaptured. The uncertainty of what comes next in this scenario is a breeding ground for fear and agitated emotions.

Thus, for a smoother transition from independence to dependency, and in order to temper isolating and confusing feelings, start each day with a pledge to your parents that you're there to support them through all of these changes and you will ensure their safety. If they're able to maintain a calm demeanor, this will allow you to remain calm, too.

On this subject, Leon Brown offers the following words of wisdom: *"Be patient. Life will offer you another chance as soon as you find calm within, for abundance is born out of calmness."*

## DUALITY: BURDEN OR BLESSING?

Duality, or the idea of opposing thoughts, is one way to view and better understand the world. For example, how can you understand the concept of light until you've experienced the dark? Thus, it's the comparison of the two ends of the spectrum that allows you to recognize and comprehend your circumstances.

Through the lens of duality, you may categorize events as good or bad. However, in truth, *every event in life is neutral, and it's only the individual who colors it with emotion and proclaims it good or bad.*

Nonetheless, life is rarely lived in stark blacks and whites; mostly it's lived in varying shades of gray, which makes it black and white at the very same time. It's your perspective which allows you to see your life one way or the other; for example, you can look at a liquid-filled glass and see it half full or half empty.

It goes to show you that everything in life is about your perception. Thus, you have the ability to regard the frailty of your parents and their need for your care as a burden, a blessing, or a mixture of burdens and blessings.

## LOVE VS. FEAR

*Love vs. Fear* is one of the greatest dualities that occurs on this planet. When distilled down to the most basic of levels, these two are the only emotions that exist and every other one stems from them. If you can accept this idea, it will be a lot easier for you to start understanding your emotions and why you feel and say some of the things that you might later regret.

When you see the world through the eyes of love *(and I'm not talking romantically but being able to see the positives in life)*, good feelings are created. This allows you to feel peaceful and content. You believe the world is a safe place and that you can attain your desires. This spills over onto your relationships and, consequently, you feel more generous and considerate towards others.

Conversely, when you see life through the eyes of fear, you feel everything is conspiring against you; in fact, you probably feel that you just can't get a break. You may believe you're being punished somehow and may even query why bad things are happening to you when you've tried so hard to be good. It's important to understand that God, the universe, or a higher power in which you believe didn't pick you out and say: *"Ah ha! Let's get him or her."* That kind of thinking is a victim's mentality in operation.

To understand this concept further, let's take a closer look at what operating in fear really means. Consider the seven deadly sins, which consist of greed, lust, pride, anger, gluttony, jealousy, and sloth. If you examine your feelings about any of these, you will discover that fear lives very close to each of their surfaces.

Here are a few possibilities.

1. If you are experiencing feelings of greed, jealousy, envy, or lust, these can be indicative of being fearful of not having enough.

2. If you are experiencing angry feelings, you could be afraid of change or of losing something or someone.

3. If you are experiencing prideful feelings, you may be afraid of not being enough. Thus, you show off and act supercilious to hide those feelings.

4. If you are experiencing feelings of sloth, you may be afraid of failure so you give up before encountering obstacles or defeat.

When you operate in fear, it causes a physical reaction to occur in your body, often referred to as *fight or flight*. There's also a third possibility: you can *freeze*. In all three of these instances, it's really hard to know what to do.

1. In *flight*, you deny that there's something wrong. You don't feel capable of dealing with it, so you may ignore it or not admit to yourself that a problem or issue exists.

2. In *fight* mode, you're angry. In this state of "seeing red" nothing productive can be accomplished.

3. And when you're *frozen*, you are unable to act, move or think, so you do nothing.

## Words of Assistance, Comfort and Inspiration

When your parents are aging, needing more care or when diagnosed with an awful disease such as Alzheimer's, it's very frightening and the unknowns of it are daunting.

Consequently, at first, you may do all three – flee, fight (or rail against), and freeze. All of these are very natural reactions when you experience a foreign-to-you obstacle. You do yourself a disservice, if you beat yourself up for feeling this way.

Everything in life is a process and, when you skip some of the phases, things have a tendency not to make sense. Often you have to go back to the beginning and repeat several of the steps to straighten yourself out. Therefore, you can see that addressing your grief opens up the path to an introspective journey where you have an opportunity to utilize a *step-by-step procedure* that allows you to slowly examine your belief system.

On this journey, you may frequently realize that some of the things you believed, or thought to be true, are not true anymore. Next, you have to figure out what you're going to do about it and how you're going to integrate your new thoughts into your life so they can best serve you and the ones you love.

## HOW TO RECOGNIZE ANGER

Anger is probably the most common fear-based reaction you will experience when dealing with situations concerning your aging parents.

*No doubt about it.* It's scary when your parents take a turn for the worse. Without realizing it, your reaction to the fear surrounding this situation may be expressed as anger. Again, this is very natural.

What I'd like you to do is to take a moment and look beneath your anger so you can determine of what it is you are afraid. *This is the path to learning how you can appropriately respond to it.* After all, if you don't know the root cause, it's pretty difficult to take proactive steps to change your behavior and figure out a resolution.

*So what are some possible reasons why you're afraid, which, in turn, causes your anger to escalate?*

1. Before it consciously dawns on you that something must really be wrong with your parents, you may be angry at them for being stubborn, not remembering, for wandering off, or for accusing people of stealing their things when you know very well they have hidden them. However, subconsciously, you're starting to get worried, although a common reaction is total frustration at this turn of events, which, in turn, elicits anger.

2. Deep down, you may be afraid that, if this aberrant behavior is occurring in your parents, it could also happen to you. It's sort of self-serving and that's okay. Whether you think you're evolved or not, human

beings are basically egocentric. This is not necessarily a bad thing, for it doesn't have to be selfish in nature. In fact, it's a critical trait – otherwise why would you, for example, take care of yourself, get a job, or look for love. You're trying to get your needs met and when you don't – *what happens?* Well, you're not a happy camper and you rage at the world. So, it's always a good thing to consider your own feelings towards a situation to help you determine an underlying cause.

3. You may also be afraid of what a caregiving situation might mean to your life. You question, for example, what changes you might have to make and the affect it will have on your emotional and economic stability or if you might have to share your home and give up some of your time and privacy.

If you can step away and consider some of the preceding thoughts, you will be able to see that you're not really angry; you're afraid and your *reaction* is anger.

Now, HOW do you turn your natural reaction into an appropriate response? *I'm sorry to tell you that it's not that easy.* It requires a conscious decision and lots of practice. And, be aware, as much as you try, you're human so be prepared to accept the fact that you're going to fail sometimes.

Before I address how you can turn your reactions into appropriate responses, I want to touch briefly on the concept of neutrality that I mentioned previously. This concept is at the foundation of understanding *how* you approach the circumstances you encounter *determines* whether your result will be of benefit or not to you and your loved ones.

## NEUTRALITY

In the section labeled *Duality: Blessing or Burden*, I stated that every event in life is neutral and that it is only the individual who colors it with an emotional connotation and makes it a positive or negative experience.

*Now, don't get me wrong.* This does NOT mean you should forego feeling your emotions. It's actually quite the opposite; the only way to resolve an issue is to face and feel the painful emotions you are trying to avoid. That is how they are processed through your body and eventually released. For example, when you finally accept that you parents can't live alone or you can't avoid dealing with the ramifications of a tough diagnosis such as Alzheimer's, your emotions are all over the place. Matter of fact, they are fluctuating wildly.

To better understand this concept, close your eyes and think of a pendulum that swings back and forth. Now, reach out and grab that pendulum and hold onto it as it completes its natural back-and-forth motion. That's you experiencing the rollercoaster of your emotions. To make it more confusing, as you swing, you may be looking down into the dark abyss of not knowing what to expect or what to do next.

*However, what do all pendulums finally do?* That's right; they stop. They come to rest in the middle, or what I call neutral. While you were swinging, you were processing how you felt about the situation – which could include coming to terms with your own mortality now that your parents are ill. That's really not a good time to think of appropriate resolutions for issues confronting you because you're too emotional, which can cause faulty and foggy thinking.

When you reach neutral – which is when your emotions calm down and you jump off the pendulum to land on solid ground – you're able to get a handle on your situation or gain a clearer perspective. You can begin to look around and see possibilities and take non-emotional forward moving actions that allow you to deal with the situation at hand.

If you noticed, I mentioned a really important word: *non-emotional*. That doesn't mean you've stopped loving your parents or that you don't feel badly about both your and their situation. But, if you're the one who has to make some hard choices or, out of all your siblings, you're the one who is hands-on with your parents on an everyday basis, you're doing yourself a disservice if you stay on a high emotional plain every moment – or if you continue to swing on that pendulum. I don't know about you, but that would make me sick to my stomach!

So, my sisters, who are very supportive and will let me vent to them about my frustrations, also live across the country and *maybe* see my mom once a year. It's gotten to the point that it's hard to talk to her on the telephone, so they don't even speak much between visits.

*What about me?* I visit my mom between one and three times a week, sometimes more often, if there's a specific issue; solve all her problems; and take care of her finances. I participate in programs with her and make sure she feels cared for and safe. While one of my sisters, especially, freaks out over every little thing and tells me, *"You're so strong; I don't know how you do it,"* I don't have the luxury of being at the mercy of my emotions while still remaining sane and able to operate in my own life AND deal with my mother's issues.

I can't just *talk* about being strong. In fact, I'm not that strong; I'm simply doing what needs to be done because, if I don't, then it won't happen.

Thus, when I suggest that you attempt to be *non-emotional* in dealing with some of your caregiving tasks, I'm not telling you to be cold and cruel-hearted. I'm simply letting you know that you must protect yourself because you won't be of any use to you or anyone else, if you jump off the "crazy bridge" every time an issue arises.

Here's the bottom line: *it's necessary to learn how to operate in neutral so you can respond and not react.*

## REFLECTIVELY RESPOND VS. REFLEXIVELY REACT

This section heading is a little bit of a tongue twister! Think about it like this: you want to *reflectively respond*, or think before acting or saying anything you might later regret, vs. *reflexively react*, which is acting or saying things without forethought. *Sounds great, but let me tell you this is easier said than done.*

The most often time people react is when their expectations and reality don't mesh. For example, when you change roles and you become the parent and your parent becomes your child, this is not what you *expected* to happen. It upsets the natural order of the world, and this confusing circumstance leads to fear, which is often expressed as anger.

You can think of *reflexively reacting* as a natural impulse. For example, if I push you (figuratively or physically), what do you want to do? You probably want to shove right back or, when someone pushes your buttons *(and your parents know where all those live)*, you usually react with an outburst of some sort.

Unfortunately, most often this situation concludes in a less than desirable outcome. Therefore, the trick is to *first* determine the result you want and *then* take the appropriate actions in order to reach your goal. That's the definition of *reflectively responding*.

As I mentioned previously, this is a learned trait that takes lots of practice. And even then, you're human so you're not going to get it right all the time. That's okay! If you can remain consciously aware of your words and actions, each time you practice the art of responding, it becomes a more natural way for you to conduct your life.

This is a concept that you can take to heart to help you in your other personal relationships, as well as in your professional ones.

Let this be one of your goals in your often-frustrating interactions with your parents: *to learn how to respond vs. react.* In turn, this will allow you to feel more peaceful and create the most benefit for your parents.

## W.H.A.M.!

Your caregiving responsibilities live in duality because they are both a burden and blessing at the same time. It is very easy to get caught up in the burden side of this situation *vs.* focusing on the blessings that are evident, even in the worst of circumstances. In order to avoid getting bogged down by negativity and to learn how to appropriately respond, it's important to keep certain things in mind.

Here is an easy mnemonic device to help you accomplish this feat.

### THINK W.H.A.M.!

#### W = WHY

It's important to determine **WHY** you have decided to offer your caregiving services. There are many possible whys, which could include the following: your naturally helpful demeanor; your desire to honor your parents; your love for your parents; the feeling that you need to "repay" the support your parents provided to you; your feelings of responsibility; or the lack of other options.

When faced with challenging conditions, it's quite easy to "forget" why you've put yourself in this difficult and trying situation. Therefore, you might want to come up with a daily reminder with which you can start each day. It could be as simple as repeating the mantra, *"I love my mother"* or *"I love my father."*

You can extrapolate this idea to a romantic relationship, too.

To keep the fires burning in a long-term relationship, it's important to find something that makes you fall in love with your partner each day. In essence, you're "reminding" yourself why you love him or her. These don't have to be grand gestures; it could simply be a look, a shared smile, or a silent knowing. It's the same for your parents; you can remember happy childhood memories and specific times when they provided loving support that helped you to become who you are today.

## H = HOPE

The next step in unearthing the hidden blessings of caregiving is to find **HOPE**. Hope is not always easy for caregivers to keep alive because you know the progression of Alzheimer's encompasses pain for you and your loved one. Moreover, it's an illness that ends in lots of small deaths and eventual demise.

In most instances, people will tell you to look at the big picture. Well, in this instance, I believe it's beneficial to do the opposite: *look at the small picture*. This makes your hope attainable. For example, it may be unrealistic to hope your parents will remember how to complete many of the tasks of life, but it may be attainable for you to hope that you can enjoy a serving of ice cream together, which may stir up happy memories of long ago and leave you both feeling content in the moment.

## A = ACTION PLAN

After deciding for what you are hoping on a specific day, come up with an **ACTION PLAN** to ensure it can come to fruition. This plan entails detailing the steps you're going to complete in order to turn your hope into a reality. For example, if you are hoping to make your loved one laugh or smile on a particular day, a beginning step of your action plan may include finding a simple joke or recalling and sharing a funny story from your childhood. Additionally, you could share pictures that capture the funny antics of your children or grandchildren. If you're childless, consider locating pictures of pets in funny poses. Surfing the Internet can provide you with many options.

*Here's a more practical example.* If your hope for a specific day is that your loved one will be able to brush his teeth, your action plan might include prompting the necessary actions *vs.* doing it for him. The steps associated with this plan could include encouraging him to locate the toothbrush; rinse the bristles; apply the toothpaste; brush the teeth in a prescribed manner; rinse the mouth; rinse the toothbrush; and store the items when done. While you brush your teeth mindlessly, for someone who has "forgotten" how to do this task, you need to carefully lay out the procedure.

Another option would be to silently brush your teeth alongside your parent in an attempt to ingrain the correct sequencing. This would enable him to mimic the step-by-step procedure without the added confusion of too many words and instructions.

## M = MECHANISMS

To help you respond *vs.* react, you will also want to develop **MECHANISMS** which will allow you to better cope with frustrating situations. A very useful mechanism is a *mantra*, which is a simple statement that can help you to gather your thoughts, ignite your patience, and keep you on an even keel.

Caregivers can think of a statement or saying that they can repeat to themselves in their moments of difficulty or when they are having trouble facing the perceived burdens of the day. Repeating a mantra allows you to breathe deeply and to respond in a calm manner *vs.* reacting in anger and frustration.

The simplest of mantras is the one I previously mentioned: *I love my parents.* Additionally, you may want to add the following: *and I want them to feel safe and cared for.* By silently and repeatedly reciting this statement, you're afforded the time to decide what kind of response you would have to make in order for them to feel safe and loved. I'm sure you'll agree that it certainly wouldn't be anger.

Keep in mind that some of the preceding concepts I've discussed might be ones with which you're not familiar. In fact, you may even be hearing about them for the first time. Since I've just painted broad strokes here, you will probably need more time to digest them and investigate their validity. Furthermore, perhaps, some of what I've said hasn't resounded with your spiritual belief system. Please know that I'm simply giving you food for thought and presenting a different perspective from which you can view your circumstances.

In all my writing and speaking, I always tell people that they must listen and/or read with discernment and then pick and choose what sounds right for them. I hope you will do the same.

## Mom's Story

With the preceding information as a foundation, the next sections will focus on some of the practicalities of caregiving. To begin with, I'm going to share a little bit of my mom's story, which will allow me to illustrate how to take the concepts I've explained and apply them to your own situation.

As of this writing, my mom is 94 years old and physically very healthy. College-educated and extremely smart, up until she was 86, she was very independent and lived on her own. As an only child, when her parents became ill, she cared for both of them. Due to the challenges of this situation, she never wanted or expected her four children to feel obligated to care for her. Consequently, she encouraged us to be autonomous, and we all left the familial nest to pursue our own dreams. This search took us to the four corners of North America – New York, Canada, the Pacific Northwest, Arizona and, upon their retirement, my parents moved from New York to Florida.

When my widowed mother was 85, a hurricane blew through Florida and destroyed her home and, subsequently, disrupted her life. In retrospect, I believe it caused her to suffer from Posttraumatic Stress Disorder, which, in turn, hastened her journey towards Alzheimer's.

As my sisters and I all lived far away, the depth of the havoc wreaked upon my mother by that fateful storm eluded us for quite some time.

After the storm, we each took turns going to Florida to help her manage this distressing situation. However, in the immediate aftermath of the hurricane, she came to stay with me for a month. Although she could have remained in Arizona for a longer period of time, she was quite anxious to go home and contend with the damage her home had sustained.

While determining whether her apartment was salvageable, friends welcomed her to stay with them in their homes. As time progressed, it was established that it wasn't safe for her to return home due to mold damage. Moreover, it would take an excessive amount of time and effort to rebuild, which was something my mother did not have the energy to attend to by herself. Thus, we proceeded to assist her in securing a new apartment, which was not far from her original location.

Unfortunately, she encountered difficulty adapting to all these changes and different environments. She also was without most of her belongings as the storm had destroyed eighty-five percent of them.

Soon, it became an almost everyday occurrence that she would call one of us to report that something inexplicable (to her) had taken place. At the top of the list was she insisted that her new landlord was coming into the apartment when she was out and stealing her things. We, of course, had no reason to doubt her and reacted accordingly. *After all, why wouldn't we believe her?* We always knew her to be level-headed and logical. We even went as far as confronting the landlord who nicely told us that this situation was *not* occurring and perhaps my mom was having issues to which we should attend. At first, we didn't believe the landlord (or didn't want to); unfortunately she was one hundred percent correct in her assessment of my mother.

## Words of Assistance, Comfort and Inspiration

As an aside, when she was finally diagnosed with Alzheimer's, the doctor said if her house hadn't been destroyed, and she wasn't so upset and confused by all the moves, her symptoms would have been kept at bay for many more years. The reason for this is that the memories of where things were in her house, how to drive to the grocery store and her other usual haunts, and how to go about her daily tasks of life were embedded so deeply that she could function by rote. However, when she moved to a different area and a home where her belongings were placed in different drawers and closets, she couldn't remember what she was supposed to do and where her things were located. One of her "logical" conclusions was that someone must have stolen her possessions.

*This is something to keep in mind.* If circumstances indicate that a move is necessary from one state to another so that your parents can be closer to you, remain aware that it's a very big adjustment for them to leave everything to which they've become accustomed. Moreover, it can be so overwhelming that your parents may never regain their bearings, which is what happened to my mother.

To handle her confusion, my mom started making up stories. I came to learn that this coping mechanism has a name: it's called *confabulation* and it's a mechanism used that allows you to fit the story to fit the facts of your perceived reality. Her story was pretty simple: things were missing, so someone must have taken them. Next, she became stuck in this story, and it turned into her new truth. Nothing could convince her of any other possibility, even when the items were later found. She would curb fit that result by believing that the thief decided to return certain items.

Although I'm sure Mark Twain wasn't trying to explain confabulation, I think he nailed the concept when he wrote the following passage.

> "When I was younger, I could remember anything, whether it had happened or not; but my faculties are decaying now and soon I shall be so I cannot remember any but the things that never happened. It is sad to go to pieces like this but we all have to do it."

Our initial reaction – and a very understandable one – was to query: *"What is going on?* and *"Why does she insist on arguing about this?"*

My sisters and I would furiously burn up the telephone lines with questions such as the following: (1) *"Do you think she's making this up to get attention?"* (2) *"Do you think she's safe? What if this really is true and someone is terrorizing her."* and (3) *"Oh, she's so stubborn; why won't she believe us when we've investigated the situation and found her accusations to be unfounded?"*

Both frustration and anger began to arise in both my mom and us. She was upset that we seemingly didn't believe her, and we were upset that she wasn't listening to us when we presented her with what we believed to be irrefutable facts about the status of her goods. It was a no-win situation.

To compound the problem, we were operating at a long distance, which made it difficult to determine the real truth. We wavered between worrying that the accusations against the landlord could be true *vs.* feeling frustrated that her confusion was self-imposed because she insisted on hiding her valuables and, subsequently, forgot where they were stashed.

My mom's car was also damaged in the hurricane and had sustained hundreds of scratches. Paranoid tendencies started to boil, and she came to believe that a neighbor, who she accused of taking some of her things, was also marking up her car. She insisted that every night he would sneak down to the parking lot of her complex and add a few more scratches to the car. When we asked her why she believed that this man was driven to pursue her so relentlessly, her answer was *"Because he wants to drive me crazy."*

Trying to allay her fears, when we each spent time with her in Florida, we took pictures of every scratch. When she asserted that there were new ones, we pointed out on the pictures that they were already there. Nevertheless, her belief that this was a real occurrence continued and nothing we did or said could change her mind.

Even after she moved to a new complex, which was gated and security-manned, she maintained that this 70-something man was climbing over the gates every night at midnight and damaging her car. She became so agitated that she started parking it far away from her apartment to try to fool him. Despite the difficult feelings that arose when we saw our mom acting like this, we still had to applaud her for her craftiness and the extremes to which she went to protect her property.

*Finally*, it was starting to dawn on us that a serious problem existed and something was very wrong. We realized that we needed to take the appropriate response to protect her from the demons she thought were pursuing her, *even if we knew them not to be real.*

Now, you might wonder why it took us so long to come to this conclusion. The truth is that everything becomes crystal clear when you look at it in retrospect and can fit all the pieces of the puzzle together. However, you're only able to make decisions and discern the whole picture when you have ALL the information in front of you.

Individually, the majority of these incidences seemed manageable because they were occurring slowly. My mother also had no desire to leave Florida and everyone and everything she had known for the past thirty years. Consequently, our pleas to have her move closer to one of us fell on deaf ears. This was quite understandable, so we tried to provide assistance while accommodating her wishes until the evidence became too overwhelming to ignore.

So, you can see how my sisters and I swung on that pendulum about which I told you. We became angry, frustrated, scared, lived in denial and felt every emotion in between. It's only AFTER we experienced all these emotions (and reactions) that we were able to move closer to neutral, which allowed us to spring into action and pick the best course of action.

At times, it's easy to process your emotions quickly and get to your response in a matter of minutes. Other times, it takes longer because you don't realize what's going on right away. It's important to gather all your facts as well as allow yourself to feel your feelings. It's only then that you'll be able to determine how to appropriately respond.

*Words of Assistance, Comfort and Inspiration*

## It Doesn't Have To Be Alzheimer's

My family's response was to move my mom from Florida to Arizona where I reside. This was the most natural of choices, since my sisters live in cold climates and my mom had become accustomed to the warmth and easy living of Florida. Moreover, my temperament was probably the best suited to be able to deal with the issues that were arising.

Moving your parents closer to you or another family member might be the best course of action for your family, too. However, it's also important to keep in mind that every time your parents act out of character, the reason for the disruption doesn't have to be something dire such as Alzheimer's Disease. Consequently, it behooves you to thoroughly investigate other possibilities, especially before instigating a move that can compound issues.

You may not be familiar with the concept of *the collective consciousness*, which is a set of shared beliefs and moral attitudes that operate as a unifying force within society. What that means is that your thoughts are linked together with everyone else's thoughts, and this creates the reality you know. In essence, no man is an island and everything you think and do affects this collective.

Currently, there is a lot of attention on Alzheimer's Disease. In fact, most of the baby boomers I know panic each time they forget where they left their keys or can't recall a word for which they are searching. They might jokingly call it a senior moment, but lurking behind that euphemism is the question they secretly ask themselves: "Am I having Alzheimer-like symptoms?"

The greater the societal focus on the memory loss factor of Alzheimer's, and the more we each think and worry about it, the more the idea is perpetuated that equates forgetting or misplacing something every so often to the development of the disease. The real truth is that a waning memory is part of the *normal* aging process and is *not* necessarily indicative of Alzheimer's or another form of dementia.

Some other typical age-related changes that may have you questioning your mental health include the following.

1. You make a bad decision ... once in a while

    *Conversely, in a person with Alzheimer's, poor judgment is often exhibited along with the prevalence of impaired decision making skills.*

2. You forget to make a payment ... once in a while

    *Conversely, in a person with Alzheimer's, there is the inability to manage money, to construct a budget or to work with numbers in general.*

3. You forget the day of the week but recall it shortly thereafter

    *Conversely, in a person with Alzheimer's, the day, month, year or season is forgotten or confused and passage of time remains a mystery.*

4. You have trouble finding the right word to use ... once in a while

*Conversely, in a person with Alzheimer's, there is difficulty following or joining a conversation, and often items are named incorrectly.*

5. Misplacing or losing an item … once in a while

   *Conversely, in a person with Alzheimer's, there is a misplacing of things and a subsequent belief that they are stolen or, after an item is lost, being unable to logically retrace steps in order to locate it.*

If your parents are exhibiting troubling behavior, or it seems like they are worsening in the area of memory loss or the other areas mentioned above, there are other avenues to check out before jumping to conclusions or self-diagnosing.

*Dementia-like symptoms can be the result of any of the following.*

1. Under-active thyroid

2. Vitamin deficiencies

3. Too much calcium

4. Clinical depression

5. Viral and/or bacterial infection

6. Lead/mercury poisoning

7. Schizophrenia

8. Syphilis that has spread to the brain

*Unaddressed hearing loss* is also a rather large overlooked area of concern.

Unable to hear correctly, seniors often misunderstand questions and answer incorrectly. This could lead you to falsely conclude that they are more confused than what is actually true.

Seniors often put off attending to their hearing loss for as long as twenty years, so say some professionals. One study indicates that as many as 27 million Americans who are 50+ in age and two-thirds of men and women older than 70 have some degree of hearing loss. Unfortunately, when hearing loss is not remediated with hearing aids, a cognitive slide commences.

*The following are some ways to recognize if your parents are exhibiting a hearing loss, although not admitting to it.*

1. They turn up the volume to high on the television and radio.

2. When trying to listen while conversing, they might put their hand by their ears in a cup-like fashion.

3. They give inappropriate or wrong responses to simple questions or to questions for which you already know the answer.

4. When trying to listen, they might turn their head or lean forward towards the speaker.

5. They stop participating in well-loved activities that require listening to a group leader/other members or responding to questions.

6. Uncharacteristically, they start to mumble or speak unclearly.

7. They shy away from using the telephone because with-

out visual clues they can't understand the conversation.

Two other important areas of concern to which to pay close attention are the development of *urinary tract infections* and *dehydration*, which in older adults can be deadly and often set off a chain reaction of bad things. In fact, after the age of 65, dehydration is one of the most frequent causes of hospitalization.

Since sixty percent of your body is made up of water, and you naturally lose more than eighty ounces of water daily just through normal activities, it's imperative to stay hydrated in order to ensure that your body can function at an optimal level.

*Here's why a problem frequently arises.*

1. Aging can cause people to lose their sense of thirst. When water consumption exists at a minimal level, this often leads to the development of persistent urinary tract infections.

2. Age also slows down your metabolic rate and you need fewer calories. Furthermore, you're not as active, so your appetite decreases and that's an issue because almost everyone gets about half their daily water requirement from solid food and fruit and vegetable juices.

3. Your fluid balance is also affected by health problems common in elderly adults, such as high blood pressure, diabetes, and heart disease, as well as the medication taken to counteract these maladies.

4. Aging bodies also have difficulty in regulating their core temperature. Consequently, seniors perspire less, so it's harder to keep cool and they can become easily overheated. In turn, they become dehydrated and this can lead to heat exhaustion and heat stroke. When you become dehydrated, there's not enough fluid in the body to carry blood to all the organs.

*You may not be aware of the fact that many of the signs of dehydration are virtually identical to senile dementia symptoms.*

The most common signs and symptoms of dehydration include the following.

1. Persistent fatigue

2. Lethargy

3. Muscles weakness or cramps

4. Headaches

5. Dizziness

6. Nausea

7. Forgetfulness

8. Confusion

9. Deep rapid breathing or an increased heart rate

Other less common signs and symptoms of dehydration can include the following.

1. Excessive loss of fluid through vomiting, urinating, stools or sweating

2. Poor intake of fluids

3. Feeling like you can't keep anything down

4. Sunken eyes

5. Dry or sticky mucous membranes in the mouth

6. Skin that lacks its normal elasticity and sags back into position slowly when pinched up into a fold

7. Decreased or absent urine output

8. Decreased production of tears

**Here's how you can apply the preceding data and turn a natural reaction into a response.**

Before I became aware of these facts, when my mom would seemingly act more confused than usual, my first reaction would be to say to myself, *"Oh no, she's getting worse!"*

Next, I'd jump off the crazy bridge and imagine what that could mean to her and to me. However, with just a little amount of information, I was able to take a pause and remind myself that the possibility of an underlying physical cause existed. If this were the case, it might also be something which could be easily remedied.

This allowed me to quickly pull myself back in order to respond. Now, my first response is to call her doctor, and he usually orders a UA (urine analysis) to rule out an infection and/or dehydration.

## READJUSTING THE LENS

When your parents start acting out of character, it's time to readjust the lens from which you view them. Here's one hard truth you must come to accept: *They are no longer the same and are not capable of thinking and doing things as they once did.* If you don't adjust your expectations, disappointment and frustration are sure to follow.

It's NOT that they are forgetting things. *It's that they have actually forgotten how or lost their ability to remember.* Think of it as if their brain is a computer on the fritz. Thus, they are able to word process in the moment, or able to converse, but both the save (remember) or print (able to retell) functions no longer work.

Here's another way to try to comprehend their mental capacity. For those of you who know about how sales of stock are recorded, two methods are utilized: LIFO, *when the last stock purchased is the first one recorded as sold* vs. FIFO, when the *first stock purchased is the first one to be recorded as sold.*

When it comes to those with Alzheimer's, they are operating under the principle of LIFO, and instead of FIFO, their memories are also subject to the principle of FILO, which is *First In, Last Out.*

In simple terms, what this means is that old memories are the last to go (FILO), and new memories simply don't stick (LIFO). This the reason why your parents can remember perfectly what happened when they were 30 or 40 but can't recall what they had for lunch – or if they even ate lunch on a particular day.

To further understand this concept, be aware that there are also different kinds of memory that are affected by Alzheimer's.

They include the following:

1. **Episodic Memory**. This controls the ability to comprehend and learn new information, as well as remember recent events.

2. **Semantic Memory**. This controls the ability to recognize, name and categorize items. *This is the reason why someone with Alzheimer's often misnames a common object, even as they point to it.*

3. **Procedural Memory**. This controls the ability to remember the steps to take in order to complete a task. This is one of the last areas to be affected by Alzheimer's. *Therefore, your parents may still be able to complete some of the daily tasks of life by rote because the procedures have been so deeply ingrained.*

4. **Working Memory**. This controls the ability to concentrate and the short-term retention of necessary information, for example, remembering the address where one lives.

## How Memories Are Made

Knowledge of the different types of memory allows you to better understand (and accept) why it's possible for your parents to remember their childhood but not what happened yesterday. In turn, this can help to lessen your frustration.

Memories are formed in a two-step process.

1. The first step is completed by the hippocampus portion of the brain. When you experience something or learn something new, the hippocampus recognizes it and, subsequently, registers it and sends this new information to other parts of the brain to be stored.

2. When you remember something, you are actually retrieving the memory from these other portions of the brain.

Scientific research indicates that the hippocampus is one of the earliest sections of the brain damaged by Alzheimer's. Accordingly, when it's impaired or in the process of dying, it *never* registers the event or the new incoming knowledge. Moreover, since the information is never registered, it isn't able to send this 'non-existent' message to be stored elsewhere.

This fact makes it *impossible* for the person afflicted with Alzheimer's to retrieve this information because there's nothing there to access. Therefore, your parents act the same as if the event never happened. Thus, the identical questions are asked repeatedly and you get blank stares if you say, "*I just told you about this a few minutes ago.*"

*Words of Assistance, Comfort and Inspiration*

It's important to learn how to handle your frustration with repetitive story telling because it is going to be something with which you are faced during every interaction.

The brain of a person with Alzheimer's simply lacks the ability to do its job properly. Consequently, no matter how hard you try, you cannot teach, incessantly remind, or compel your parents to stop repeating themselves.

## A Mechanism For Handling Repetition

Knowing *why* your parents can't stop repeating themselves, doesn't make it any easier to have the same conversation many times over. However, *at least* if you understand the physical reason why it is impossible to stop it from occurring, it can stem your frustration.

Every time you're listening to a story for the umpteenth time or answering the same questions, one option is to repeat the following mantra.

*This is the first time that
my mother/father is hearing this information.*

This enables you to keep a smile on your face and to avoid letting an annoyed voice creep into your tone that urges you to say: *"I just told you that – don't you remember?"* Well, NO, they don't!

## LEARNING TO SPEAK A NEW LANGUAGE

In addition to dealing with the issue of repetition, it's also necessary for you to learn to speak a new language to and with your parents. Furthermore, it's important to learn how to decipher their new way of communicating because of their difficulty with proper word finding. The latter skill has taken me a few years to master. You'll discover that it's easier when you're speaking to them in person because you can utilize visual cues; however, on the phone, it becomes quite a challenging task!

When parents have lost a great deal of their ability to communicate verbally, keep in mind that it's still possible to connect with them through their other senses.

1. **Touch**. *A warm hug, squeeze on the shoulder or an outstretched hand communicates loving feelings, which can make your parents feel safe.*

2. **Taste**. *You can provide your parents with a meal of comfort food or a sweet treat that says I love you.*

3. **Smell**. *Strong fragrances have the ability to stir memories, so you might bring your parents a bouquet of their favorite flower. Additionally, if they had a garden, you might locate a fragrant item that has the ability to spark happy times they spent in this venue.*

4. **Hearing**. *Sing a familiar song to your parents, or record a CD that contains songs from the era of their youth.*

5. **Sight**. *Reminisce with old family photos that are familiar and comforting to them. If they had a hobby, such as sewing,*

*share items of theirs that you may have as keepsakes.*

If your parents are still able to carry on a conversation, here are four pitfalls to avoid.

1. ***Avoid Pointing Out That They Are Wrong or Mistaken About Something.*** If your parents don't remember something correctly, allow them to save face by not contradicting or correcting them – unless it's something dangerous or detrimental to their health. If they are still cognizant enough, they'll recognize their mistake and be embarrassed. If they're not as aware, it will still feel like a scolding and nebulous unpleasant feelings can be generated.

2. ***Avoid Arguments.*** This is a no-win situation when speaking to people who have dementia. They have lost the ability to think logically and, no matter how many times you explain your position, it cannot be comprehended or processed. Instead, attempt to divert their attention elsewhere as you guide the conversation in a different direction. Soon, the disagreement and previous heated discussion will be forgotten.

3. ***Avoid Asking If They Remember Something.*** As described in a previous section, those with Alzheimer's have lost the ability to remember. Consequently, avoid embarrassing or frustrating them by asking questions that they have no ability to answer. Rather than asking questions that begin with "Do you remember when …?" – instead, make statements that begin with *"I remember when we did X … and it was sure fun!"* Then they simply can agree – even if they don't recall the particular incident.

**4. *Avoid Unpleasant Topics That May Upset Them.*** Often, people with dementia forget that some of their loved ones have passed away, for example a beloved spouse. They wonder why this person doesn't visit and, if you tell them because he/she is dead, they may become very upset. After all, no matter how many times you tell them this news, each instance is essentially the first time they are hearing about it. Now, if they directly ask you if the person is deceased, you should tell the truth. However, before they become more upset, attempt to direct the conversation elsewhere.

Depending on how in-depth your conversations are, you may also want to avoid other topics that may upset them or start an argument. A good example of this is politics. Again, you're not going to convince them of anything nor will they be able to logically comprehend why you believe you're right and they are wrong.

In general, keep conversations light and attempt to create an atmosphere where your parents feel safe and loved.

Recapping, here are ten tips to keep in mind when visiting those with Alzheimer's, whether it be your parents, another family member or a friend.

1. To appear non-threatening, make eye contact and wear a smile. If a person is in a wheelchair, bend down so that you're at his/her level.

2. State your name and your relationship. For those who may not recall who you are, it may be upsetting if

you said you were a daughter or a son, for example, and your parent didn't remember that fact. In this case, simply say hello and state your name.

3. Speak in short sentences and use simple vocabulary.

4. Speak in a calm and soothing voice.

5. Don't bombard the person with questions, one after the other. Allow there to be plenty of time for the collection of thoughts.

6. Refrain from arguing or correcting mistakes made.

7. A planned activity, no matter how short, will make the time spent together less awkward. It can be as simple as applying lotion on the hands or arms. Touch is always comforting.

8. Don't make any sudden moves towards this person. In case you need to awaken him or her from a nap, gently rub the arm or shoulder. If the atmosphere is friendly, you might offer a gentle hug as a greeting and farewell.

9. Avoid discussing controversial topics.

10. Reminisce about the past *vs.* chitchatting about the present or future.

## PARANOIA

In my opinion, paranoia is one of the most difficult issues to address. You have to remember that you're thinking rationally and the Alzheimer's patient has lost that ability.

Along with the hippocampus being damaged, the prefrontal cortex also degrades over time, and it's this portion of the brain that controls logical thinking.

Consequently, while something may seem so simple and clear to you – which makes it easy for you to logically understand an event or even dismiss it as inconsequential – these same situations that Alzheimer's patients encounter are complex and very confusing to them.

At the earlier stages, they are having a fear-based response, too. For example, they're cognizant enough to realize their memory is slipping, which causes them to have difficulty recalling where their possessions have been placed. This is a very frightening thought, and it's certainly easier to dismiss or deny it.

Accordingly, they create scenarios to explain missing items. For example, it's much easier to blame someone else *vs.* to take personal responsibility, which would mean they would have to admit something is wrong. Early on, my mom was aware enough to say *I'm losing my mind*. Now, she insists she remembers perfectly and that I must be wrong – or, worse yet, that I don't believe her.

*What are some specific steps that you can follow in order to counteract the paranoia?*

1. Since arguing won't get you anywhere, it's not necessary to agree or disagree. Instead, you can say, *"I'm sorry you feel that way."* By phasing your response in this manner, you avoid negating their beliefs and feelings, but you also aren't agreeing with them, for example, that someone stole their possessions.

2. Next, redirect the conversation with a statement such as *"I'll look into it to figure out what's going on and let you know."* This will most likely satisfy them until the next time they become agitated about the same subject. Rinse and repeat!

3. The next step is to figure out how you can mitigate the issue or try to remedy the situation so it stops reoccurring. For example, when my mother was in an Independent Living complex and various employees had keys, she insisted someone was coming into her apartment and stealing her things.

*To make her feel safer, I took several actions.*

a. I installed an extra deadbolt lock to which only she and I had the key.

b. I also installed a spy camera that was pointed at the front door, which was the only place of entry. If she said something was missing, I would go through the footage with her to show her that no one had entered the apartment.

c. I also consistently encouraged her to leave things out on the counter or the dresser, which made it less likely that she would hide an item in an undisclosed and mysterious place.

d. I also took pictures of all her possessions so that I would have proof that everything was the way she left it with nothing disturbed or missing.

Each of these attempts worked for a while until she would come up with a new story to prove that "someone" was taking her things that she couldn't find (and had hid). Usually, I could find the items, but she was very good at squirreling away things in the most unlikely places. Eventually, you'll discover all these places as I did and finding the items will be a much easier and less frustrating task.

It's natural to be emotional about the deteriorating condition of the mental status of your parents, and you will most likely experience the highs and lows that come with this event. However, if you are going to be caregiving on an everyday basis, it will be difficult for you to retain your own sense of equilibrium, if you react with extreme dismay over each incident.

Although to an outsider it may seem a bit harsh, approaching your parents' care with a more clinical attitude may be your saving grace.

Embracing this coping mechanism doesn't mean that you have stopped loving your parents. This is far from the truth.

In fact, by adopting this type of attitude, you are better able to deal with the hard decisions to be made and the aberrant behavior that may be exhibited. It would be very difficult for you to function well in your own life, if you constantly let your emotions be in charge.

As with everything, there is a proper time and place to feel and express your emotions and a time to keep them in check.

## LET A THERAPIST BE THE BAD GUY

If you suspect that your parents have a mental ailment, it's important to find a neuropsychologist to conduct a psychological evaluation rather than relying on an internist or general practitioner.

Additionally, if you think your parents would benefit from talk therapy, find someone who is trained in geriatric issues rather than a generalist. If your parents are on Medicare, you have the option of also speaking to a psychologist. As long as your parents have seen the doctor first and your appointment is about your parents and the difficulty you're encountering with the situation, it will be covered under their policy.

*Here's an added benefit of starting a relationship with a psychologist that I discovered.*

Even though I delicately broached the subject with my mother that I thought it prudent for her to move from an independent living facility to an assisted living one, she protested. This was a perfectly natural reaction, for no one would willingly want to abdicate the little independence she still retains. I had a plan, though, and this first conversation was merely to introduce her to the idea. In response to her reluctance to move, I tabled the conversation and said we would go visit her doctors and see what they thought about the idea.

Our first appointment was with her primary geriatric physician, who concurred with me. In truth, he was the one who encouraged me to start seriously thinking about a move. Next, we went back to the psychologist she had seen a couple of times, who, of course, also concurred.

They both explained to her that their only goal was to make sure she was safe and well taken care of. The best way to ensure this was to move to an assisted living facility where she would be able to receive extra help with the daily tasks of life.

Both doctors were more than willing to be the "bad guy" in this scenario. As I initiated the move, each time she protested, I referred back to the fact that I was only following her doctor's orders and that I couldn't disobey what they deemed a necessary medical measure.

# Words of Comfort and Inspiration

This section provides you with fifty inspirational and comforting thoughts for your consideration.

Each offers a change in perspective, which, in turn, can help you to deal with your loss and allow you to start recognizing the blessings in your burdens.

# INTRODUCTION

While the preceding pages focused on providing a mixture of facts and theory to help you understand loss and how feelings of grief impact your caregiving, in the following pages, I will attempt to inspire you by providing a change in perspective.

Here's the thing that I can't do for you: *make a conscious decision and choice to move forward and recognize and accept your own limitations as a caregiver.* That job belongs to you, and I hope you'll accept that position because that is one of the best ways to handle this situation.

And, while you're taking the appropriate steps to come to grips with your new circumstances, keep in mind that you can only do your best. However, it's when you're confronted with issues and problems, such as dealing with a dire illness, that a golden opportunity lies in front of you to learn about life and deepen your relationships.

Do try to refrain from comparing your efforts to others, though, for each situation and relationship is unique. As Dick Sutphen said, *"Everyone is doing the best they can – not the best they know how, but the best they can."*

This experience is building up your emotional muscles, which will serve you well in the future. As you move through your life, you'll be confronted with the need to make choices all of the time, not just in a caregiving situation. Some will be small and inconsequential, and others will be big and impactful.

In all instances, when you *reflectively respond*, choice comes before action because you've thought through a plan on how you will go about achieving your goals. It's imperative to consciously decide how you're going to choose to respond to your circumstances, today and each day that follows.

As you formulate your responses, keep in mind that the tone of your language and the words you will use are very powerful. R.M. Engelhart reiterates this thought in the following statement.

> *"Words make a difference.*
> *They can create and destroy.*
> *They can open doors and close doors.*
> *Words can create illusion or magic, love or destruction."*

I invite you to please enter the door I am opening to you with my words of comfort and inspiration found within these next pages.

## MORE THAN MERELY EXISTING

If your parents or another loved one has been diagnosed with Alzheimer's, you're in the process of losing an important relationship, which may have been the basis for you to soar in other areas of your life. Now that this foundation is being cruelly ripped away, you may feel as if you're simply existing – slithering along the ground day-by-day like a caterpillar. The view from this place is very narrow, and it's difficult to see what lies ahead. Perhaps, even when you decide to raise your head for a moment, all you see are big feet (read: issues/problems) ready to squash you.

I ask you to consider the following words of Jewel Diamond Taylor, who said: *"Your thoughts, words, and deeds are painting the world around you."*

Of course, you're mournful over your circumstances, and it's important to take the appropriate time to grieve. However, there also comes a point when it's time to shift your thoughts towards the positive. This allows you to be grateful for what you DO have *vs.* mourning what is missing.

When you're able to start modifying your attitude, the landscape of your life will also shift. Instead of slithering on the ground, you can begin to test your wings again and see the view from a higher perch. As Rumi states, *"You were born with wings. Why prefer to crawl through life?"*

Let's read about how you can learn to fly!

## IT'S A NEW GAME

Peter Drucker said, *"The greatest danger in times of turbulence is not the turbulence; it is to act with yesterday's logic."*

Becoming a caregiver changes the backdrop of your life. Moreover, your life is a new "game" that has new rules. What previously worked for you has been irrevocably altered. If you keep applying the same precepts, you most likely will be met by obstacles as you attempt to accomplish your goals.

Instead, take a deep breath, step back for a wider view, survey the new terrain, and afford yourself the time to learn the new language and customs of this land. Look for the potholes upon which you may trip. Take some time to map out your "trip" before you dive in head first.

Yesterday's logic is your old normal. Now, you are living and must adapt (and adopt) to your new normal.

Furthermore, don't be thrown by the term "new normal." Normal is just an illusion – a label attached by others who have decided what is normal for them and not necessarily for you. Moreover, normal is always in a state of flux as you grow and change through your life experiences.

## WHAT KIND OF ADVICE ARE YOU RECEIVING?

In Lewis Carroll's book, *Alice's Adventures in Wonderland*, Alice and the Cheshire Cat have the following conversation.

> Alice asks the Cat: *"Would you tell me, please, which way I ought to go from here?"*
>
> *"That depends a good deal on where you want to get to,"* said the Cat.
>
> *"I don't much care where,"* said Alice.
>
> *"Then it doesn't matter which way you go,"* said the Cat.
>
> *"So long as I get SOMEWHERE,"* Alice added as an explanation.

If you are an inexperienced caregiver, it's possible that you're receiving plenty of advice on how to handle this new situation, including things you *should* and *should not* do. At times, it can be overwhelming, and the truth is that your situation (which includes the type of relationship you have with your parents) is unique to you.

While you digest your new circumstances and duties, you may want to take a note from Alice and just keep moving *vs.* getting stuck or stagnating in negativity. You'll eventually get SOMEWHERE and, when you get there, you'll figure out if it's the place you want to be. If not, you'll keep putting one foot in front of the other until you get to a better place.

Here's an exercise for you to try that can assist you in processing your feelings. Recite the following list of phrases aloud and think about how each one makes you feel. Each represents a different level of thought. While some are limiting beliefs, others are empowering.

Which one will you choose to say today?

I COULD *embrace my caregiving duties with joy*

I CAN *embrace my caregiving duties with joy*

I WOULD *like to embrace my caregiving duties with joy*

MAYBE *I'll embrace my caregiving duties with joy*

I SHALL *embrace my caregiving duties with joy*

I MUST *embrace my caregiving duties with joy*

I SHOULD *embrace my caregiving duties with joy*

I HAVE TO *embrace my caregiving duties with joy*

I WANT TO *embrace my caregiving duties with joy*

I WILL *embrace my caregiving duties with joy*

I AM GOING TO *embrace my caregiving duties with joy*

I EMBRACE MY CAREGIVING DUTIES WITH JOY

*Note: You can replace the phrase "embrace my caregiving duties with joy" with lots of other phrases, such as: let go of negative thoughts; release my tight grip on my dashed expectations; feel good; feel hopeful; love myself; stop feeling resentful; stop feeling angry, etc.*

## TAKE CARE OF YOURSELF

I recently read an article for which Richard Cohen and Meredith Vieira were interviewed. For those who are not aware, Richard (Meredith's husband) has Multiple Sclerosis. Here is a snippet from the interview, which conveys an important message for all caregivers to take to heart.

*"Patients and caregivers need to believe in themselves.*

*We all stand at intersections or sit in coffee shops and overhear other people talking and I wish I had a dollar for every time I've heard someone say in any context, 'Oh, I couldn't ever deal with that' or 'I couldn't possibly cope with that.'*

*I want to turn to them and say 'How do you know? You're probably much stronger than you know. How do you know you wouldn't rise to the occasion?'*

*I think that people sell themselves short.*

*People have a reservoir of strength and resilience that is invisible to them. It's something that they cannot see, but it's available to them and I think that if people believe in themselves and their strength a little bit more, the rest can fall into place – whether it's getting through a bad time or whether it's confronting a doctor, both of which can be daunting.*

*Both are doable; people just have to believe in themselves enough."*

Both Meredith and Richard refuse to see themselves as victims of their circumstances. Despite the challenges they face, both individually and as a family, they refuse to cower and give up simply because it's hard.

Moreover, they don't see their life as horrible; it's simply their life and they live it the best they can – snatching up moments of joy when they are presented and accepting help when it's needed and offered.

Your life may not be the life you imagined you would be leading, but this is the one you have been given. It's up to you on how you will view your circumstances and how you will respond to them.

## MAKING IT ALL BETTER

People who experience difficult times long to be compassionately understood – for someone to acknowledge their pain *vs.* simply offer empty words in a feeble attempt to try to make it *all better*. In truth, it's a very long journey to *all better* and to find this place requires lots of hard work, not just wishful thinking that your bad feelings will magically dissipate.

Of course, "all better" is a tricky term, especially the ALL part. Even in the place where you find happiness and feel *better*, you will still wish your loved ones could be well and there to share it with you. That's natural, so you don't have to work so hard to let go of this thought. However, it doesn't negate the fact that your changed life can still be magnificent in its own unique way.

*Let's talk about compassion for a minute, though.*

Many friends and family members might not have the emotional capacity to support you in your plight or to even attempt to assist you in feeling better. They may seemingly reject you because it's too hard and heart wrenching to stand by and witness a person for whom they care experience pain.

Although this is disappointing, to enhance your understanding about how these people might feel in the wake of your difficulties and loss, consider the following thoughts of Henri J.M. Nouwen.

Furthermore, while applying these to your interactions with your parents, *if you're being especially hard on yourself*, attempt to also exhibit a little self-compassion.

"Let us not underestimate how hard it is to be compassionate.

*Compassion is hard because it requires the inner disposition to go with others to the places where they are weak, vulnerable, lonely, and broken. But this is not our spontaneous response to suffering. What we desire most is to do away with suffering by fleeing from it or finding a quick cure for it.*

*Compassion asks us to go where it hurts, to enter into the places of pain, to share in brokenness, fear, confusion, and anguish.*

*Compassion challenges us to cry out with those in misery, to mourn with those who are lonely, to weep with those in tears.*

*Compassion requires us to be weak with the weak, vulnerable with the vulnerable, and powerless with the powerless.*

*Compassion means full immersion in the condition of being human.*"

## CONTROL IS AN ILLUSION

After you fully confront what lies ahead of you and, in turn, this causes you to deeply grieve for what once was, you may feel that you've lost control of your life.

*In truth, control is an illusion to which most like to cling.*

Before your time of difficulty, you might have been lulled into believing that you were at the helm of your life and could be in charge of every detail and how it would proceed. Now that this illusion has been ripped away, you know that EVERYONE is at risk for having his life disrupted.

I know it's painful to face this real truth. Personally, I was very happy living in my fairy tale bubble of a life before my loss cruelly pierced it. However, due to that awakening, I know that now I'm more aware of the possibility of future losses so this makes me cherish each moment in the present.

If you can recognize this fact, too, it will make both of us so far ahead of the game than most. It's important for you to put that knowledge to good use as you move forward on your journey through life. A good place to turn to for some inspiration is nature. Its cycles of loss and rebirth are a constant reminder that, no matter the barrenness of the landscape, regeneration is always close at hand.

I like what Jeffrey McDaniel said about the seasons: *"I realize there's something incredibly honest about trees in winter, how they're experts at letting things go."*

In the winter, when the trees "let go" or release their leaves that have browned or died, they move into a hibernation phase. In essence, they have cleared their plate to make room for what comes next. They rest and wait for the sunlight to warm them and stimulate new growth.

You, too, are resting in your grief – going underground, so to speak. While in this phase, work on releasing negative emotions, so you can make room for more joyous ones to warm your soul.

## FINDING YOUR POWER

Abraham Hicks suggests the following: *"As you begin to state what you do want – rather than clamoring about what you don't want – you come into your own power."*

This statement reflects the journey of caregiving, which is one that can take you from the depths of darkness to the light of renewal. At first, you're justifiably angry that this is your life. You don't want it, and you may even wish you could go to sleep and upon wakening have it revert to its previous condition.

Unfortunately, as hard as you wish, the only way life can be lived is going forward. As you take on new tasks and complete them successfully, you empower yourself. With introspective thought, you can figure out who you are and what you want. In turn, this grants you more empowerment.

When you experience loss, you enter a time of transition and, as you move forward through it, it's up to you to grab onto the positives and release the negatives. It's hard and it may hurt. However, that's what growth is all about. You are being stretched to your limits and beyond.

Determine what you want and then construct an affirmation about it. Furthermore, it's more beneficial, if you affirm in the present tense with the words *"I am"* vs. *"I'm going to."* This brings the thought into the *now* where you have the ability to make it happen. Here's an example of an affirmation. Determine if it rings true for you. *"I am a confident person who is successfully demonstrating that adversity can be overcome, and I am handling my circumstances with grace and compassion."*

## SPRING ALWAYS FOLLOWS WINTER

Due to your circumstances, you may feel as if you're living in the winter of your discontent. The gloomy prognosis that has been delivered and your ever-increasing caretaking role can certainly make it seem pretty cold and dark. If you're feeling this way, I suggest that you take another page from nature's script, which says: *"No matter how long the winter, spring is sure to follow."*

When you're coping with the many medical issues of your parents, it's easy to get stuck in a space that feels cold, dark and wintery. You "bundle up" to protect yourself from outside forces that make you sad or circumstances that are too hurtful in which to participate.

Try to recall the feelings you might have on the first day of Spring, which is a great time to take a positive step forward for it is heralded as a glorious time of rebirth and renewal.

Harriet Ann Jacobs said: *"The beautiful spring came; and when Nature resumes her loveliness, the human soul is apt to revive also."* During this season, as it gets warmer outside, you begin to shed your winter layers of clothing. I request that you figuratively do the same with those feelings and behaviors that are preventing you from coping and healing.

As you continue down your path of caregiving, I ask you to continue to shed more of the layers you've worn in your winter of discontent, which may include anger, resentment or fear. If you can rid yourself of some of that extra weight, the sunshine of life will be better able to penetrate the depths of your soul.

## Procrastination Gets A Bad Rap

It's so easy to recognize the clear path for others to follow – and even easier to tell them what to do and how to do it! However, when it comes to yourself, at times, it's easy to get stuck in the overwhelming demands of daily life, which, in turn, can muddy the path to your goals.

Additionally, you can become frustrated or less hopeful, and this mindset can hamper your progress, too. Lastly, when something is hard, or if it's something you perceive as not pleasurable, you tend to find a myriad of other things to do first.

Although procrastination usually gets a bad rap, it doesn't always have to be a dire course of action. In fact, at times, it can be the best course of action.

*Think about it.* Rather than impulsively jumping into a situation, when you procrastinate a bit, you allow yourself the time to gain perspective, learn about yourself, establish better balance and boundaries in your life and heal completely from past wounds. Of course, you need to remember to temper this tendency, so you can avoid becoming completely frozen with inaction. Eventually, it will become necessary to move forward in some fashion.

Keep in mind that it's a rare occasion that everything about a situation will be perfect before it becomes necessary to take that first baby step. Perfection is highly overrated anyway!

## Past, Present, Future

It's very easy to get trapped in your memories of the past and how things used to be. Let's take a moment to examine your past, as well as the present and the future.

If you will, imagine your past, present and future like three pieces of paper all tied together with a string running through the middle of each. If you were to pick up one end of the string and dangle it in the air, the papers would not fly away for they are inextricably connected – one leading to the next.

Although they each have an impact on the other, Marcel Pagnol states, *"The reason people find it so hard to be happy is that they always see the past better than it was, the present worse than it is and the future less resolved than it will be."*

When you remember the PAST, it's easy to block out the negatives and recall only a rosy picture. Although, it's great to remember your past glowingly, try not to romanticize it so much that the present pales in comparison to it.

In the PRESENT, with so much to do and so little time, it's very easy to get caught up in the minutia of your life. You can become vulnerable to a sense of being overwhelmed or not be able to see the forest for the trees.

Keep in mind that you will encounter ups and down in every era of your life. At times, it's important to step back and put current difficulties in perspective so you can figure out the best way to move through them.

And then there is the FUTURE. If you're always worrying about the future – and this leads to chronic indecision and subsequent procrastination – you can freeze in place and end up avoiding any forward moving action. This, in turn, can lead to more worry.

In essence, you've created a vicious circle that is of no benefit to you. So, although I said in the last section that procrastination gets a bad rap, you also have to learn to temper it and find the right balance between it and total inaction.

While it's a very good idea to always keep an "eye" on the future and move forward towards your goals, it's equally important to live in and enjoy the present moment before it speeds by – never to be recaptured again.

Cherish all the small moments of joy you can find with your parents. The only time that is promised to you and them is now.

## What Lies Beneath The Iceberg?

*Have you ever heard of the term "iceberg beliefs"?* These are powerful thoughts that float beneath the surface of your consciousness, which can significantly undermine your resilience and cause you to overreact to a particular situation.

A good majority of these thoughts are born in your childhood psyche and the interactions you witnessed in your familial home. So, if you grew up with the message that life is a series of calamities (which you *won't* be able to overcome), when you are confronted with difficulty, you may panic and not know which way to turn.

Another iceberg belief that may have been ingrained in your psyche is that *"you're neither good nor smart enough."* Consequently, as you confront new situations, you don't feel qualified to resolve them successfully.

As you move through your grief and sense of loss about the difficult times your parents (and you) are encountering, consider looking beneath the surface to see what iceberg beliefs you might be harboring. Next, do your best to melt down those fortresses of stubborn beliefs that could be hampering your success.

*What's one thing you can do to move this process forward?* Literally, simply take a few steps!

**Although this is certainly not medical advice and you should always check with your own medical professional before embarking on any type of exercise program,** research has shown that (for many) improving your mood can be accomplished by starting a regimen of a brisk 30-minute walk three times a week.

Furthermore, this practice has been shown to be just as effective as taking antidepressants because exercise increases the release of endorphins and serotonin, which are the same chemicals upon which this type of medication has an effect.

Both exercise and meditation put you in a "zone," which is the high you feel after about twenty minutes into a session of either and has to do with the increase in the release of alpha waves. Alpha waves produce peaceful and relaxed thoughts, and, in fact, Dr. David Simon says: *"The most direct and consistent way that I know to bring peace into every aspect of your life is through the regular practice of meditation."*

If you're intimidated by meditation, it's not as complicated as you may believe, and it doesn't have to involve you sitting cross-legged and whispering "Om." In fact, you can meditate (which in its purest form is really only clearing your mind) while you walk. Just keep your eyes open and watch where you're going!

For simple instructions on getting started with the practice of meditation, please visit the following link.

*http://www.understandingspiritualityfromatoz.blogspot.com/p/meditation-made-easy.html*

## LIFE ISN'T BLACK AND WHITE

J.D. Stroube shares his belief that *"life is filled with unanswered questions, but it is the courage to seek those answers that continues to give meaning to life. You can spend your life wallowing in despair, wondering why you were the one who was led towards the road strewn with pain, or you can be grateful that you are strong enough to survive it."*

Consequently, as much as you may want definitive answers on various issues, including how to cope with your new circumstances, most often you have to settle for some shade of grey resolution. Life is simply *not* lived in black and white. Matter of fact, it's quite often black and white at the very same time! However, that doesn't mean your answers must remain elusive.

Although you may not be practiced in trusting yourself, the truth is that you already intuitively know what is involved in reaching a resolution or finding a solution. One of the lessons of dealing with difficulty is that it teaches you how to recognize your own truths by listening to your gut. As you get better at this, you will be able to pull your answers from your subconscious and act on them.

I like what Avantika says on this subject: *"A day is not always bright, and nights are not always dark. All that matters is what's inside, because day and night are a reflection of you."*

What that means is that YOU have the power to change the lighting of your life.

## OPEN EVERY DOOR

Emily Dickinson wrote, *"Not knowing when the dawn will come, I open every door."*

It is the same for a caregiver. As you travel on your journey, open and step through all the new doors of opportunity that are presented. You never know who or what you will encounter and how it can be the spark that changes everything for you.

Now, if you're thinking that this "spark" has to be something momentous that will automatically make you feel better, consider the words of Ralph Waldo Emerson, who said: *"The invariable mark of wisdom is to see the miraculous in the common."*

## Filling Up That Empty Feeling

Bruce Lee said, *"The usefulness of the cup is its emptiness."* It's possible to extrapolate this concept and apply it to many areas of your life.

After determining and accepting the fate of your parents and all that it means, you most probably have an empty feeling. In an attempt to fill yourself up, at times, you may indulge in unhealthy and/or risky behaviors such as overeating or imbibing too much alcohol. Unfortunately, these behaviors don't help and, in fact, often cause a new set of problems.

Gabriel Garcia Marquez said, *"Perhaps this is what the stories meant when they called somebody heartsick. Your heart and your stomach and your whole insides feel empty and hollow and aching."*

Consequently, the next time you reach for an unhealthy food in an attempt to fill your void, take a step back and consider the idea that eating it might compound your grief. Unhealthy eating can jeopardize your health, as well as your ability to address your issues with a clear head *vs.* a foggy one laced with sugar and an overload of carbs.

Instead, try filling up your "empty cup" with healthy activities that help you to expand your body, mind and spirit. A great place to start is with developing your sense of gratitude.

I know it's probably hard to feel grateful when you're watching a loved one endure such difficulty. However, when you think about it, I'm sure you'll realize that you still have a life filled with abundance. In truth, it all comes down to your attitude and perspective.

For example, consider that you still have an open and giving heart buried beneath your sorrow – not only because you've experienced great support and love from your parents but because you also now know the pain of losing it.

You learn, grow and come to appreciate life as you experience contrasting circumstances. Life is lived on the continuum of the duality between the positive and negative. Choose to take steps that will move you closer to the light and away from the dark.

## THE GIFT OF PAIN

Samuel Taylor Coleridge wrote about the gift of pain in the following passage.

> *"Real pain can alone cure us of imaginary ills.*
> *We feel a thousand miseries*
> *till we are lucky enough to feel misery."*

Well, maybe you don't feel *lucky*, but the illness of a loved one certainly puts pain into perspective. Just think how nice it would be to simply have sore muscles or temporary inconveniences that may annoy you *vs.* knowing the devastation of having an ill loved one.

Remember this lesson of loss and don't allow the little things in life derail you from attaining your larger vision or overshadow the joy you can capture in the moment.

## LOOKING AT LIFE THROUGH NEW EYES

Anais Nin said, *"We don't see things as they are. We see things as we are."*

Accordingly, individuals hold their own perspective, which is influenced by their life experiences. After a tough diagnosis, while the world-at-large generally stays the same, it's you who changes and views and comprehends it through different eyes.

Try not to take offense at seemingly insensitive comments made by friends and/or family members. It's important to understand that these people believe they are saying and doing the right things in order to help you. However, they are basing their remarks on the way they see the world *vs.* looking at a situation from your point of view and level of responsibility towards your parents.

So, while others may urge you not to get upset about the disturbing actions of your parents, you feel tethered to your emotions, causing you to hurt when your parents hurt. The path in front of you looks covered with emotional landmines, and it's not until you can move closer to neutral that you will be able to protect yourself from the highs and lows that accompany caregiving.

It takes a long time and lots of hard work to understand that you can release the pain you're experiencing about the circumstances of your family and still retain happy memories that remind you of the love you share with your parents.

## Responding To Loss

There is virtually no one in this world who can avoid some sort of loss. Consequently, it's important to develop skills on how to respond to it in a healthy and successful manner.

Oliver Wendell Holmes said, *"If I had a formula for bypassing trouble, I would not pass it round. Trouble creates a capacity to handle it. I don't embrace trouble; that's as bad as treating it as an enemy. But I do say meet it as a friend, for you'll see a lot of it and had better be on speaking terms with it."*

Although it's true that loss is universal and inevitable, each person will react (and then eventually learn to respond) to his difficulties and grief in a unique manner.

It's not a matter of being strong or not. In fact, Ovid said, *"ALL human things hang on a slender thread; the STRONGEST fall with a sudden crash."*

You can think of it in this way – if you've lived life well and loved hard, your "fall" is more difficult because you know exactly what you've lost and understand fully the depths of the devastation you face when your loved ones are no longer able to live healthy and fulfilling lives.

## HANDLING CELEBRATORY EVENTS

When a parent no longer recognizes you, the celebratory days of Mother's Day in May and Father's Day in June can become two very difficult days for you. With activities centered around the family, it becomes glaringly obvious that some members of yours are missing or remain unaware of the date.

It may SEEM as if the possibility of happiness has deserted you. That's not true. It's still waiting for you. Keep the faith. Jacques Prevert said, *"Even if happiness forgets you a little bit, never completely forget about it."*

Even in the midst of unhappiness, it's up to you to stir happy feelings inside of you – to reignite your pilot light.

If you're not in a good place on these days and others, do something nice for yourself that can bring a smile to your face. This will perk up your muscle memories of what it feels like to be happy. Do it enough times, and it can become a natural state of being once again or, at least, you'll be able to access it on demand.

## The Longest Day

The Summer Solstice is the longest day of the year. However, in the year 2013, it came with a twist.

The *Huffington Post* reported the following statistic.

> *"While the solstice in the northern hemisphere traditionally falls on June 21 ... it will begin on Thursday, June 20, for parts of the western U.S. ... The time of the solstice depends upon your position on Earth and, as a consequence, where you are in relation to the sun."*

Isn't this reflective of how you see most everything in life? It all depends on your perspective. That's why different people can look at the same glass and some see it half full and some half empty.

You have the ability to let your times of difficulty empower you to explore the possibilities of many perspectives OR to keep you frozen in the place where you are only able to see one viewpoint.

*Which one sounds more enticing to you?* Choose the result you want and then make the appropriate choices to help you attain it.

## GROWTH

Winston Churchill said, *"Mountaintops inspire leaders but valleys mature them."* The same can be said of loss and encountering difficult circumstances.

It's a lot easier to be positive about life when things are going well and you're surrounded by your loved ones. It tests the mettle of a (wo)man when tragedy strikes and life changes in an instant. It's not pleasant, but these are the times when you grow the most.

Since, you can't change the facts of your life, make sure to wisely use this time of caregiving and make it work for your greatest benefit. Furthermore, heed Paulo Coelho's warning of: *"Don't allow your wounds to transform you into someone you are not."*

## Quizzes vs. Final Exams

Trey Parker and Matt Stone, writers of the television show *South Park,* said, *"I just realized that there are going to be a lot of painful times in life so I better learn to deal with them in the right way."*

In actuality, each disappointment you encounter is a small loss, a small death. You could consider these instances "quizzes" in the book of life, while the illness and subsequent death of a loved one may be the final exam.

These occurrences can be terrific instructional moments for your children in which you are presented with the opportunity to teach in the most powerful manner, which is by example. They can be afforded an important life lesson and learn techniques on how to overcome small setbacks in preparation for prevailing over larger issues.

## FINDING THE HARMONY

Will Durant suggests that one of our tasks in life is *"to seek, beneath the universal strife, the hidden harmony of things."*

This is good advice to take with you on your journey through the grief you're experiencing while you offer care to your parents.

Keep peeling back the layers of your sadness and grief to regain a balance in your life. Furthermore, continue to look for the uncomplicated truth that lies beneath the visible drama of your life.

## WHAT IS LIFE?

Crowfoot, a Blackfoot warrior and orator who lived in the mid 1800's, asked the question: *"What is life?"* His answer was as follows.

> *"It is the flash of a firefly in the night.*
> *It is the breath of a buffalo in the wintertime.*
> *It is the little shadow which runs across the grass*
> *and loses itself in the sunset."*

Although an individual afflicted with Alzheimer's may be physically present, you're certainly losing the person who he/she once was. Accordingly, when loss occurs, questions are often asked about the meaning of life and death.

The life your parents knew is gone (as well as your own) and, until equilibrium is reestablished, nothing makes sense. This uneasiness may set you on the path of searching for meaningful answers to big questions such as the purpose of life. Crowfoot answers this question with a simple, yet profound answer. *"It is the flash ..."*

Maybe there are no "big" answers. Rather, life is made up of an accumulation of small moments, and you need to stand in awe of them all. In view of that, go forth today and find a small moment in which to revel. Share it with others so that they may rejoice with you.

## LOOK AT THE SMALL PICTURE

The mountain of sadness and grief in front of you may look insurmountable. In turn, this can bring forth thoughts of feeling besieged by the enormity of the responsibility of caregiving.

Due to your limited attention and ability to focus, this is one time in life that it may be more helpful NOT to look at the big picture.

Instead, attempt to simply focus on the task directly in front of you. Conquer that one and THEN move onto the next.

In the following statement, the fairy tale character Rapunzel offers some good advice on how to take this concept and turn it into a reality.

*"In pursuit of our dreams, we do not always need to have fuel to take us to that destination. Sometimes we just need fuel enough to take us to the next service station and fill up."*

## Is This How You Feel?

Anne Lamott offers a great description of how the bereaved may feel at the inception of grief. She wrote, *"My heart was broken and my head was just barely inhabitable."*

If you're in the process of losing a loved one, it's very possible that you're experiencing difficulty keeping rational thoughts in the forefront of your brain. They seem to be flying out of your head as fast as you can grasp at them in an attempt to stuff them back into your brain. This is how an Alzheimer's patient feels, too.

Thus, similar to your parents, it may seem as if your thoughts can't stick or mysteriously seep out because forgetfulness reigns in your life right now.

Luckily for you, as you travel further on your journey through caregiving, one by one, you will be able to recapture your "thoughts" and this will allow you to move forward while making beneficial changes in your life.

## FINDING THAT COMFORTABLE PLACE

Mark Twain said, *"A powerful agent is the right word. Whenever we come upon one of those intensely right words, the resulting effect is physical as well as spiritual and electrically prompt."*

The word *smultronställe* may be one of those words that can bring you to a comforting place in your mind. It comes from the Swedish words 'smultron' (which means strawberry) and 'staelle' (which means spot, place or field).

Do you recall the hit song by the Beatles, *Strawberry Fields*, of which the chorus is as follows?

> *Let me take you down*
> *'Cause I'm going to Strawberry Fields*
> *Nothing is real*
> *And nothing to get hung about*
> *Strawberry Fields forever*

This is a place where you can relax and let go of your worries. Thus, this word may be used as a metaphor for an idyllic spot on earth.

When you feel your responsibilities becoming too burdensome to handle, escape to your own special smultronställe.

## Moving Toward The Light

Webster defines *to enlighten* as follows: *to give spiritual or intellectual insight or to give the light of fact and knowledge to free oneself from ignorance, prejudice or superstition.*

Figuratively speaking, a light bulb turns on in your head and you see the world through different eyes. This provides clarity of purpose and the knowledge of what's really important in life.

Dr. Wayne Dyer goes on to say, *"If I could define enlightenment briefly, I would say it is the quiet acceptance of what is."*

Throughout your caregiving journey, the preceding are the "lights" to which you will be drawn.

## FEELINGS OF LOSS WILL NOT BE IGNORED

Feelings of loss (and the grief you experience because of them) will not be ignored. Sure, for a time, you can push them away with busy-ness or deny your pain. But Horace asks, *"Why do you hasten to remove anything which hurts your eye, while, if something affects your soul, you postpone the cure until next year?"*

It's impossible to erase or remove the pain of loss from your soul without addressing it – painstakingly step by step. The only way to light and renewal is to plow through the darkness.

This is applicable *not* just to grief but to any difficult situation. In order to release undesirable feelings, you first have to deeply examine them so you know exactly of what you are letting go.

## Can You Turn Off The Noise?

Thich Nhat Hanh asks, *"Do you have the time to listen to yourself, your suffering, your difficulties, and your deepest desire?"*

When you're grieving, it's important to turn off the noise in your life so that you are able to hear your answer to questions you may ask yourself about your suffering as well as your hopes and desires.

The "noise" encountered as you walk through your day can be incessant. Banks, restaurants, grocery stores, gas stations, bookstores – they all have background music playing, along with announcements blaring from loud speakers and television screens blinking news and advertisements.

Noise is often self-imposed, too. For example, rather than getting comfortable with being alone in the silence, many turn on the television or the radio to keep them company in an otherwise empty house.

This chatter, which invades society's subconscious, can be a detrimental factor in finding some quiet time to reflect and examine your life – the past, present and the future to come.

Although it may be impossible to avoid *all* the noise in your life, you can attempt to set aside a pre-planned segment (no matter how short) each day for undisturbed introspective thought.

## WHAT IS THE TRUTH?

When you experience loss, the layers of your ego are peeled away and you stand before the world naked as a baby. Just as a baby, you yearn to learn and understand the new truths of your life. This is a part of the journey upon which you've embarked.

In the following passage, Khalil Gibran offers directions to guide you through this process of self-discovery.

*Say not, 'I have found the truth,' but rather,*
  *'I have found a truth.'*

*Say not, 'I have found the path of the soul.'*
  *Say rather, 'I have met the soul walking upon my path.'*

*For the soul walks upon all paths.*

*The soul walks not upon a line; neither does it grow like a reed.*

*The soul unfolds itself, like a lotus of countless petals.*

## Finding Optimism

Are you having a hard time feeling optimistic about your future and the circumstances of your parents?

According to Martin Seligman, author of *Learned Optimism*, optimism is a skill that can be learned and/or rediscovered. He states that, if you can focus on your character strengths (i.e. courage, compassion) rather than your perceived failings, you will be able to boost your mood and your immune system. He goes on to say that, if you can change the view of your life, you can transform it into the vision for which you yearn.

I also like what Noam Chomsky said about optimism. He states, *"Optimism is a strategy for making a better future. That's because, unless you believe that the future can be better, you are unlikely to step up and take responsibility for making it so."*

You can watch a video I recorded, accessible at the link listed below, to hear more about optimism and how you can recapture your sense of it. Consider the idea that your optimistic nature may simply be on hiatus. Therefore, to feel better about your situation, it's important to wake it up.

Winston Churchill got it right when he said, *"For myself I am an optimist - it does not seem to be much use to be anything else."*

Video on Optimism: *http://youtu.be/U2899Dh5_U4*

## IT'S NEVER TOO LATE TO CHANGE

F. Scott Fitzgerald provides a good explanation of how you can approach life through and after the experience of difficult circumstances. In truth, this is good advice to put into practice at any time in your life.

> "For what it's worth: it's never too late or, in my case, too early to be whoever you want to be. There's no time limit; stop whenever you want. You can change or stay the same; there are no rules to this thing.
>
> We can make the best or worst of it. I hope you make the best of it.
>
> And I hope you see things that startle you.
>
> I hope you feel things you never felt before.
>
> I hope you meet people with a different point of view.
>
> I hope you live a life you're proud of. If you find that you're not, I hope you the strength to start all over again."

Here's my simplified translation of the preceding: trying times that encompass loss give you an opportunity to have a do-over in your life. It's not a wanted one, but it belongs to you nevertheless. Accordingly, you might as well accept and take advantage of it.

If you can approach each day with the anticipation of a beginner, there's a good chance that you will be pleasantly surprised at what life has in store for you.

## THE MIND-BODY WELLNESS CONNECTION

As you work on healing the wound to your soul, you cannot separate the body and the mind; there is an intrinsic connection.

Maharaj Charan Singh Ji says, *"Whatever the mind does, the soul has perforce to suffer the consequences of it because the soul and the mind are knotted together."*

Henry David Thoreau agreed when he wrote, *"Good for the body is the work of the body; good for the soul is the work of the soul; and good for either is the work of the other."*

That's why it's so important to channel your thoughts to view life through a positive filter. This doesn't mean you never feel bad, it's just a general perspective you hold – that despite the hardships and sadness you encounter, you believe that everything will work out in the end (as long as you participate in forging the resolutions).

Thoughts are real energy and create your world. When you think negative thoughts, they can create dis-ease (and real diseases) within you. They emanate out and can draw more negativity to you – almost like fish hooks snagging their prey. Conversely, putting positive feelers out will magnetically draw people and circumstances to you that can help you to move out of your fog and through your pain.

Intuitive therapist Melinda Vail cautions you that the *things upon which you dwell will be the place where you dwell*. If you can corral your thoughts, you can change the topography of your life.

## IS BUSY-NESS YOUR COPING MECHANISM?

Are you using busy-ness as a coping mechanism in order to avoid thinking about the ramifications of your circumstances upon your life?

This may work for a while, but eventually you'll start to feel like a chicken running around without a head.

Moreover, this behavior also won't resolve your issues; it only pushes them aside, which isn't all bad – *if you're simply just waiting for a time when you're more able to confront them.*

I suggest that you take to heart the cautionary words of Deepak Chopra, who said: *"No solution can ever be found by running in three different directions."*

Multi-tasking often means not giving enough attention to any of your issues or projects. The result is that they all remain in limbo and nothing gets completed. Step off the crazy train; take some deep breaths and try conquering one task at a time.

## THE UPS AND DOWNS OF LIFE

If you take into consideration that there are 31+ million seconds in an ordinary calendar year, this provides lots of opportunity for you to experience many ups and downs.

If you're in the midst of caregiving and haven't yet found your stride, it's very likely that you feel your dark or down moments overpower your light or up ones. In truth, your "ups and downs" live right next to each other, and life can change from one to the other in a flash. It's your experience of the contrast between the two that allows you to understand both states of mind.

Although society generally looks at a show of weakness – *which you might believe is how you act in your down moments* – as a "bad" thing, this may mostly be because it frightens the populace. Moreover, it has been ingrained in society that people should hold in their emotions and act strong.

For a change in perspective, consider what Cecelia Ahern says about this idea.

> *"At your weakest, you end up showing more strength. At your lowest, you are suddenly lifted higher than you've ever been. They all border one another, these opposites, and show how quickly we can be altered."*

## Finding Your Courage

Sometimes, you're just plain scared about what is to come. And that's okay.

When grieving the circumstances of your parents, it's natural to get focused on the past and be frightened because you don't know what the future holds for both them and you.

Socrates offers a different way forward, which is as follows.

*"The secret of change is to focus all of your energy not on fighting the old, but on building the new."*

What this means is that it's okay to let go of the known in order to free you up to leap into the unknown. Since it may not be clear what lies on the road ahead (and most of us like to know what we're getting into before we move towards it), it's natural to be scared. Courage is moving forward despite your fears.

As you finish reading this passage, may I suggest that you pick a day in the upcoming week when you can be your most courageous self and explore a new avenue – albeit cautiously. If it doesn't feel good, you always have the option of turning around and restarting down another path. That's what experimenting in your life is all about.

## Adapting To Change

C.J. Jung suggests that *"we meet ourselves time and again in a thousand disguises on the path of life."*

This is an eloquent way to tell his followers that life flows like a river and, in order to successfully navigate the changing waters, it's important to adapt and adjust to the currents which are encountered.

At times, this river is gentle and you can float through life. At other times, especially when encountering difficulties and experiencing loss, the river runs fast and furious and threatens to overtake you. It pushes you so quickly that the landscape of your life quickly changes and you must put on a new "face" to greet and meet it.

To give yourself a small respite to catch your breath, as you tumble down the rapids into who knows what, you might look for low-hanging branches to grab or a rock upon which to rest.

During a lifetime, in every instance, you have the opportunity to learn something about yourself. Every manifestation – every disguise – it's still you, and you can integrate all of these (honed by the lessons of your circumstances) into the whole being of which you are comprised.

Don't deny any part of you. Look under your "disguises" and come to know the complete and authentic you.

*Words of Assistance, Comfort and Inspiration*

## PRICELESS!

The world today is one of intense consumerism: *Buy! Buy! Buy!* In the end, though, you won't be comforted by your things – only by the loved ones that surround you when you pass from one world to the next. Thus, it's a good decision to collect memories and not things.

Aren't your memories what warm your heart when you think of past great times you experienced with your parents and others whom you may have lost?

It's possible to continue to create more warm moments with your parents, even with their impaired state of mind. In fact, these moments are beautiful in their simplicity because they are unencumbered with any drama.

Additionally, continue to leave an imprint on the hearts and minds of the ones that YOU will eventually leave behind. The most valuable gift you can give someone is your time, attention and love.

As the MasterCard commercial goes: *Priceless!*

## Does Your Life Feel Like An Uphill Battle?

In the midst of trying circumstances, life can sometimes feel like an uphill battle. You may need to call upon your inner warrior to ward off all the slings and arrows coming at you.

However, being a warrior is more than about "fighting the good fight;" it's remaining totally aware of your circumstances so that you can respond to both danger AND opportunity.

Carlos Castaneda elegantly explains the difference in the following passage.

> *"All of us, whether or not we are warriors, have a cubic centimeter of chance that pops out in front of our eyes from time to time.*
>
> *The difference between an average man and a warrior is that the warrior is aware of this, and one of his tasks is to be alert, deliberately waiting, so that when his cubic centimeter pops out he has the necessary speed, the prowess, to pick it up."*

## IF ONLY ...

*If only ...* Is this a (wishful thinking) phrase that you've been using often?

*If only ...* we had seen the doctor earlier.

*If only ...* my parents had planned their finances more prudently.

*If only ...* I had appreciated my parents more when they were well.

You may be thinking your life would have turned out differently, *if only ....*

When you examine your life in retrospect, it's easy to compare your present reality to an optimistic fantasy of what could have been *"if only."* This type of thinking often results in the development of regrets or guilty feelings because you believe you did something wrong or missed something important.

The truth is that you are expecting something pretty unrealistic from yourself, for people are only able to make decisions with the information in front of them.

Don't let your emotions be drained by the useless feelings of regret and guilt. Instead, turn your mind to more positive pursuits and make beneficial changes in the present to create the future you desire.

Furthermore, don't burden yourself with unrealistic expectations. Difficulties most often arise when expectations and reality are out of sync.

## CAREGIVING = A TIME OF INTROSPECTION

To me, the journey of caregiving is one that is filled with deep introspective thought.

It's a time when you're able to grasp the clearest picture of your inner being because all your veils of ego have been stripped away by the trying times you're encountering.

Be courageous and allow yourself to discover the beautiful treasure that is you.

If you embark upon this journey with an open heart and mind, Eileen Dielsen lets you know what is in store for you.

> *"In the quiet depths of my soul is a mystical and beautiful world waiting to be explored."*

## You're The Star of Your Own Show

Albert Einstein said, *"Nothing happens until something moves."*

In regard to coping with caregiving duties that something is YOU!

If you want to move from Point A (which is the inception of your circumstances) all the way to Point Z (which is a renewal of your spirit), you are the one who has to take the pro-active steps to get there.

You're the star of your own show, and it's your thoughts and actions that will propel you through time and space to a better place.

## ALETHIOLOGY: THE STUDY OF TRUTH

Alethiology is the study of truth. Isn't that what loss and your subsequent actions stir inside of you? You must face the hard truths about yourself and your ability to navigate a new world.

*But what is truth?* Perhaps there are finite truths, such as the world is round and the sun rises in the morning and sets at night.

However, on a personal level, what is true can change. For example, after loss, there's a good chance that everything you believed about your life and how it would proceed has changed. And so you become an alethiologist and go off in search for your "new truth."

## UNDERSTANDING THE CYCLE OF LIFE AND DEATH

The loss of your parents as you once knew them to be, and the devastation this causes in your life, may make your friends and family to sit up and take pause.

Since man is basically egocentric, your so-called friends may keep a distance from you because your loss makes them think about their own mortality – and they don't want to or aren't able to go there.

In essence, they are not running from you but from those thoughts – although it certainly feels like desertion.

One of the lessons of loss is that you come to better understand the cycle of life and accept that death is simply one more step in that cycle. In fact, Haruki Murakami said, *"Death is not the opposite of life, but a part of it."*

And even if people avoid thinking about this, every living organism inevitably marches towards his demise the moment he takes his first breath. By addressing your thoughts and fears about death, you are better able to understand and embrace life.

## Feeling Whole Again

Torn asunder by your circumstances, it may seem as if you'll never feel whole again. Muriel Rukeyser begs to differ, though. She says:

> "However confused the scene of our life appears, however torn we may be who now do face that scene, it can be faced, and we CAN go on to be whole."

Participating in activities such as support groups and reading books by authors who have experienced similar circumstances can provide hope.

When you hear of and speak to others who have walked comparable paths, and discover how they coped and eventually found peace with the situation, it shines light into the dark tunnel in which you might find yourself.

## SHUN STAGNATION

Richard Bach says, *"Bad things are not the worst things that can happen to us. Nothing is the worst thing that can happen to us!"*

Life – *which includes your eventual demise* – continues to flow through many ups and downs as it moves you towards your purpose in life.

Just as a stoppage of water can become stagnant and start to smell, so your life can fester and eventually wither, IF you allow yourself to get stuck in negativity or become frozen with fear. You can break through your stoppages with the tools you're acquiring on your introspective journey through grief.

Take yet another lesson from nature; she shows us that there is always renewal after loss.

George Meredith said, *"Earth knows no desolation. She smells regeneration in the moist breath of decay."*

Perhaps you will only be able to catch a whiff of it when you first experience loss; however, as time goes by, the aroma gets stronger and you will be drawn closer towards it. Finally, you can become a magnificent cook and produce your own fine fragrances of a new life.

## THE DUAL NATURE OF LOSS

Death, as most every circumstance in life, exists on the plain of duality, which is the law of opposing thoughts.

That is – while death most definitely robs you of your loved ones, it often brings you closer to friends and family as they reunite to say their goodbyes and offer support.

In a moment of need, you can reach out to grab hold of those who understand your pain, who loved your loved one the way you did, and who care for you and are concerned about your well-being.

You also may be showered with love and understanding by those who have walked a similar journey of grief before you.

So while death separates you from the life you once knew, at the same time, it unites you with new companions who will hold your hand as you march towards a new life.

## REGAINING YOUR FOCUS AFTER LOSS

*If your parents have passed, did caregiving for them keep you laser-focused on the goal of providing comfort, looking for new treatments, keeping the family going, etc.?*

Now that they are gone, your focus may have collapsed and you're no longer looking outward; instead, your eyes are turned toward the ground. When in this position, it's very hard to see any opportunities that can help you to move forward on your journey.

After an appropriate time (for you), it's important to lift your head up and become aware of the world again and what it has to offer to you – as well as what you can offer to it.

Hermann Hesse wrote, *"Life is waiting everywhere; the future is flowering everywhere; but we only see a small part of it and step on much of it with our feet."*

With your new knowledge about life and death, you can take a wider viewpoint and avoid trampling those little moments you now know are so important to recognize and cherish.

## K.I.S.S. = Keep It Super Simple

Henry David Thoreau said, *"As you simplify your life, the laws of the universe will be simpler."*

The loss of a loved one rapidly clears your slate of the unimportant. As you rebuild, *Keep It Super Simple* (KISS Principle). Don't re-clutter up your life with societal concerns about inconsequential trivia that won't matter in the end. Look for and welcome new people into your life who can see through their own clutter and who get what matters most.

Applying the KISS Principle to life helps to clarify in your mind how to conquer or successfully move through all issues. It reveals the core of a matter and wipes away the outside veneer of ego and drama that can surround emotion and which is sometimes confused with logic. It also allows you to hone your listening skills so you can hear what your intuition is telling you.

If you can concentrate on what truly matters in life, the job of seeking (and finding) the correct balance (for you) of intuition and true logic (which you use to make informed decisions) will be made easier. And when you reach this plain, stop and enjoy the peaceful space you've afforded yourself where you can breathe deeply.

> *If you want to learn more about the principles of KISS, you may be interested in my book on this subject: "KISS Principles on Spirituality: 30 Ways To Find Clarity by Keeping It Super Simple." http://www.amazon.com/KISS-Principles-Spirituality-Clarity-ebook/dp/B0086GDE94*
>
> *Also available is my primer on spirituality: "Understanding Spirituality From A to Z." http://www.amazon.com/Understanding-Spirituality-Z-ebook/dp/B006WQECTQ*

## REVITALIZE YOUR ZEST FOR LIVING

In the following passage, Anais Nin, although not directly talking about grief, gives an adequate explanation of one way to process your emotions over the loss of your parents.

> "There are very few human beings who receive the truth, complete and staggering, by instant illumination. Most of them acquire it fragment by fragment, on a small scale, by successive developments, cellularly, like a laborious mosaic."

In regard to loss, it's not that one day you will wake up and automatically feel better. Matter of fact, it's more likely that one day you'll wake up and realize that, while you don't feel great, you don't feel as bad as you did yesterday.

Joy, and a revitalized zest for living, creeps back in a moment at a time. Sometimes, it's so subtle that you may even miss it as such. It's those fleeting moments when you laugh, smile, feel the sunshine on your face, or catch an ocean breeze, etc.

Try stepping out of yourself for a moment and reflect on the bigger picture of your life. Put together the puzzle of those individual moments and you may find you have more joy in your life than you realize.

# Conclusion

## Finding Grace

As a grief coach and author, I offer to clients and readers a change in perspective so that they may move through difficult circumstances with grace in order to reach a renewal of life and love. It's my fervent wish that you feel I have provided that for you in the preceding pages.

*But what is grace?*

I love this definition by Oswald C. Hoffman, who said: *"Grace is the love that gives, that loves the unlovely and the unlovable."*

In every instance, when your life drastically changes due to unavoidable circumstances, you often spend days, weeks, or months mourning the inevitable losses you're going to be forced to face. During this process, you probably don't feel very lovely or loveable. Contributing to this fact is that you may feel misunderstood and deserted by family and friends. You feel alone in your grief because no one can understand your exact pain over your loss. And so begins your unique journey of grief.

While I and others can suggest methods to work through your loss, it's you who must take an introspective journey to discover yourself and to learn to love all the parts that comprise you – the good, the bad and the ugly. The process of mourning is also one of becoming self-reliant and that is where your strength is needed most because it's hard work. It's also learning how to accept yourself, to trust yourself, to be kind to yourself, to be proud of yourself and to really come to know the stuff of what you are made.

You're shining a light into all the dark recesses of your life that you might have been able to previously avoid examining. At the beginning of this process, keep in mind that this *enlightenment* or *evolvement* is destructive because the first step is to tear away any "untruths" you've told yourself.

Once you've confronted them, it's then that you will be able to move to higher ground where you can bask in the light of understanding what is most important in this life, which is *to love and be loved*. In truth, it's your relationships that count the most; the rest of life is simply taking care of the details.

Consequently, even if you find it difficult, nurture your current relationships and open your heart to the new people who you're encountering on your journey. They've come into your life to help you or you're supposed to help them.

As you travel the road of life, and through the ups and downs you will meet, hold the wise words of Anais Nin in your heart: *"Each contact with a human being is so rare, one should preserve it."*

# Author Bio

Ellen Gerst is a Grief and Relationship Coach, author and workshop leader who helps her clients and readers to change their perspective in order to move gracefully through life circumstances to find success and a renewal of their zest for living and loving.

She is the author of several books on grief and relationships, as well as topics that include: spirituality, caregiving for aging parents, fitness and weight loss, networking and social media for entrepreneurs, teen pregnancy prevention, building confidence and the importance of a positive attitude.

Titles include: *Suddenly Single: How To Find Renewal After Loss; 101 Tips and Thoughts on Coping with Grief; How To Mourn: Help For Those Who Grieve and the Ones Who Help Them; Love After Loss: Writing The Rest of Your Story; If You Want To Be Terrific, You Need To Be Specific; Available Choices for Dating After 35+; Figuring Out Life and Death: Musings, Stories and Questions About Suicide; How To Thrive and NOT Just Survive; Lighten Up and Smile: The Power of Positive Thoughts; Mastering The Art of Intimate Relationships;* and *Thin Threads of Grief and Renewal* (co-editor).

Titles from her A to Z series include: *Understanding Dating and Relationships From A to Z; Understanding Grief from A to Z; Understanding Spirituality from A to Z; Understanding Fitness and Weight Loss From A to Z: Understanding Dementia and Caregiving For Your Aging Parents from A to Z* and *Understanding Networking and Social Media for Entrepreneurs From A to Z.*

## CONTACT INFORMATION

Connect with Ellen and find out more about her products and services via her websites.

1. Main Website Dedicated to Grief and Relationships
   *http://www.LNGerst.com*

2. Website Dedicated to Spirituality
   *http://www.UnderstandingSpiritualityFromAtoZ.blogspot.com*

3. Website Dedicated to Caregiving
   *http://www.CaregivingForAgingParents.blogspot.com*

4. Connect on Facebook for dating and relationship tips
   *http://www.facebook.com/FindingLoveAfterLoss*

5. Connect on Facebook for tips on coping with grief
   *http://www.facebook.com/WordsOfComfortToPaceYourJourneyOfLoss*

6. Find Books on Amazon
   *http://amzn.to/w27mnt*

7. Find Books on Barnes and Noble
   *http://bit.ly/LK5SJz*

Made in the USA
Middletown, DE
23 May 2016